The Epilepsy Diet Treatment

Treatment

An Introduction to the Ketogenic Diet

SECOND EDITION

THE EPILEPSY DIET TREATMENT

AN INTRODUCTION TO THE KETOGENIC DIET

SECOND EDITION

John M. Freeman, M.D.
Millicent T. Kelly, R.D., L.D.
Jennifer B. Freeman

From the Johns Hopkins Pediatric Epilepsy Center

demos vermande

Demos Vermande, 386 Park Avenue South, New York, NY 10016
Printed in the United States of America

Cover design by Sue Nordhaus

Library of Congress Cataloging-in-Publication Data

Freeman, John Mark.
  The epilepsy diet treatment: an introduction to the ketogenic
diet / John M. Freeman, Millicent T. Kelly, Jennifer B. Freeman. —
2nd ed.
          p.   cm.
  Includes bibliographical references and index.
  ISBN 0-939957-86-8 (softcover)
  1. Epilepsy in children—Diet therapy.   2. Ketogenic diet.
I. Kelly, Millicent T.   II. Freeman, Jennifer B.   III. Title.
RJ496.E6F69   1996
618.92'8530654 — dc20

                                                        95-53864
                                                        CIP

Important Note to Readers

This book is meant to introduce the ketogenic diet to physicians, dietitians, and parents of children who might benefit from the treatment. This book is not intended as an instruction manual. It cannot take into account the specific needs of any individual patient. Like any course of treatment for epilepsy, a decision to try the ketogenic diet must be the result of a dialogue between parents and their child's physician. Parents should not initiate this diet except on the advice and under the close supervision of a physician.

OTHER TITLES BY JOHN M. FREEMAN, M.D.

Seizures and Epilepsy in Childhood: A Guide for Parents, Baltimore: Johns Hopkins University Press, 1990.

Tough Decisions: A Casebook in Medical Ethics, New York: Oxford University Press, 1987.

OTHER MATERIALS AVAILABLE ON THE KETOGENIC DIET

Videotapes:
- *Introduction to the Ketogenic Diet: A Treatment for Pediatric Epilepsy* (for the entire family)
- *The Ketogenic Diet: A Treatment for Pediatric Epilepsy: A Kid's View*
- *The Ketogenic Diet: A Treatment for Pediatric Epilepsy: Doctor's Version*
- *A Primer in Calculating and Administering the Ketogenic Diet: A Dietitian and Nurse's Point of View*

For copies of all videotapes, contact The Charlie Foundation to Help Cure Pediatric Epilepsy, 501 10th Street, Santa Monica, CA 90402.

KETO 2.00 COMPUTER PROGRAM: For copies, contact the Epilepsy Association of Maryland, 300 East Joppa Road, Suite 1103, Towson, MD 21204 (410) 828-7700. Computer disks are available to parents only on referral by a physician.

KETO KLUB NEWSLETTER: to receive or contribute, write to Keto Klub, 61557 Miami Meadows Court, South Bend, IN 46614.

Additional copies of this book may be obtained from Demos Vermande, 386 Park Avenue South, New York, NY 10016, (800) 532-8663.

CONTENTS

FOREWORD

On March 11, 1993, I was pushing my son, Charlie, in a swing when his head twitched and he threw his right arm in the air. The whole event was so subtle that I didn't even think to mention it to Nancy, my wife, until a couple of days later when it recurred. She said she had seen a similar incident. That was the beginning of an agony I am without words to describe. Nine months later, after thousands of a variety of epileptic seizures, an incredible array of drugs, dozens of blood draws, eight hospitalizations, a mountain of EEGs, MRIs, CAT scans, and PET scans, one fruitless brain surgery, five pediatric neurologists in three cities, two homeopathists, one faith healer, and countless prayers, Charlie's seizures were unchecked, his development "delayed," and he had a prognosis of continued seizures and progressive retardation.

Then, in December 1993, we learned about the ketogenic diet and the success that Dr. John Freeman and Mrs. Kelly have been having with it at Johns Hopkins Hospital as a treatment for kids with difficult-to-control epilepsy. We took Charlie there, he started the diet. Charlie has been on the diet for almost two years. He is seizure-free, drug-free, and a terrific little boy.

If we had had the information in this book fifteen months earlier, a vast majority of Charlie's $100,000 of medical, surgical, and drug treatment would not have been necessary, a vast majority of Charlie's seizures would not have occurred.

The publication of the first edition of *The Epilepsy Diet Treatment* was supported by The Charlie Foundation so that other children and their parents and doctors who struggle with this problem can be informed about the ketogenic diet as perfected at Johns Hopkins. We hope this book will help others decide whether the diet is a viable alternative to their current treatment, and know that it will be a valuable guide once the ketogenic diet has begun.

Jim Abrahams, Director
The Charlie Foundation to Help Cure Pediatric Epilepsy

PREFACE

The ketogenic diet consists of heavy cream, butter, fats, a very limited amount of protein and vegetables, and virtually no starch or sugar.

"Yuk!" is the common response to this description of the diet. It is the common response of parents and, indeed, of many physicians who have not had experience with the ketogenic diet. The very concept of a mere diet being able to control otherwise uncontrollable seizures is anathema. In this time of high technology and new designer drugs for whatever ails you, even in an era when diet books are on the nonfiction bestseller lists, a diet originating from the efforts of a faith healer to control epilepsy seems counterintuitive. And yet. . . .

At Johns Hopkins we have used the ketogenic diet for decades. We have found that about 70 percent of children with intractable seizures who are put on the diet, children who often are retarded and have severe brain damage as well, will have their seizures dramatically improved. Some have their seizures completely controlled. Some have their medications decreased or discontinued. Some are able to permanently discontinue anticonvulsant medications, avoiding the inevitable side effects while remaining seizure-free, and return to a normal diet after two to three years of the ketogenic diet's rigor. If the ketogenic diet were a drug, it would probably be the treatment of choice for difficult-to-control epilepsy.

The ketogenic diet should only be used under close medical supervision. The decision to use it should be the result of a dialogue between parents and physicians. But perhaps it is worth looking beyond the initial reaction of "Yuk!" to understand what is involved and what are the benefits and consequences of a decision to use, or not to use, the ketogenic diet.

John M. Freeman, M.D.

ACKNOWLEDGMENTS

What I spent is gone
What I kept is lost
But what I gave away
Will be mine forever.

(Author unknown)

I DEDICATE THIS BOOK to the many colleagues, associates, parents, and students who have encouraged me to record my vast experience in providing instruction and counseling for children with seizures.

Millicent Kelly

THANKS TO THE MANY wonderful patients and parents who taught us the secrets of the ketogenic diet. To our colleagues Eileen P.G. Vining, Diana Pillas, and Cathy Park. Thanks especially to the Callahans, Chadwicks, Davises, Fadnesses, Hargroves, Huffmans, Herritys, Rippers, and Slinkers for their contributions. Robert Zmuda and Richard Chadwick converted their experience with their own sons into a computer program with the assistance of Sam Hundal. Our techniques and inspiration owe a lot to Dr. Samuel Livingston, who practiced the diet at the Johns Hopkins Hospital for decades before we arrived. Special thanks to Jim and Nancy Abrahams and The Charlie Foundation, whose enthusiasm was a galvanizing force.

This second edition would not have been possible without the dedication and perseverance of Cathy Park, our nurse–clinician, who has helped so many patients and parents over a tumultuous time, and whose hard work brought this edition to fruition.

John M. Freeman
Jennifer B. Freeman

Overview

Section I

Introduction to the Ketogenic Diet

MEGAN'S STORY

Dear Dr. Freeman,

I want to share with you and your team the wonderful changes in Megan's life since she has been on the ketogenic diet.

As you remember, we were having very serious and frightening prospects as a family.... Megan's seizures, which we called "stares," were out of control in spite of using three drugs. She was experiencing so many an hour that she was regressing both in school and in her personal skills. She would be unable to remember what she had been doing prior to a "stare," and therefore had difficulty staying focused on tasks—whether keeping her place in her reader or even dressing herself, or just remembering what she went to get in another room.... Being only ten years old, she was very frightened because she was not able to stop "staring," and children teased her. She cried because she would wake up at night and not realize she was in her own bedroom. She also described many auras in which she reported seeing flashing lights and people's faces changing colors....

We could not increase the Depakote level because of the side effects to her stomach. She was taking Mylanta three times daily just to coat her stomach to tolerate the Depakote. And still her stomach hurt, resulting in poor appetite—which ... had reduced her weight to the tenth

3

percentile for her age group. This constant concern over her eating patterns and small consumption had also created tension in our family over meals.

The ... seizures also resulted in her ... sleeping at least twelve to thirteen hours out of each twenty-four, including sleeping an hour at school midday.

As a result of all these physical changes, the disorder now took Megan's social life. Since she had to go to bed so early, she couldn't go to church or ... school functions. On Saturdays, she could play only in the morning because she would sleep in the afternoon. Spending the night with a friend became out of the question because she didn't get enough sleep—which increased the "stares." Her neurologist recommended Johns Hopkins Hospital and your team because he felt surgery would have to be considered—that Megan would likely become worse .... And so we came, expecting to have to chance even losing her life in order to give her the chance of improving quality of life—and save the very essence of our spirited, enthusiastic, loving child.

Due to the complexity of Megan's neurological situation, you did not recommend surgery, but offered her something incredible—a diet! You told Megan she could use her strength to turn down sugar from her friends and to stay on her diet. We will never forget how her little face lit up when you said, "no surgery."

Her life has literally turned around from that day. ... She has been very dedicated to learning about labels with sugar, preparing foods, etc., and is determined to stay on her diet.

It has been and will be worth the extra time it requires to plan and prepare the meal plans. She has had only two "stares"—one the day of dismissal from the hospital, the other at school when she began decreasing the Dilantin level.

She has really had a learning spurt. Her reading teacher ... tested Megan and ... confirmed the improvement in reading already! Megan is thrilled to be promoted to a harder reader. Her memory also improved, and she is being assigned more difficult words. She is choosing her clothes and dressing herself with little supervision from me. She is going to slumber parties!

Family and friends say over and over they can tell how well she is doing. Her thoughts are well-connected in conversation. Megan says, "I'm so much better than before I went to Baltimore. I can remember things now. I'm doing great!" In short, she is alert and happy.

After seven and a half years of dealing with frequent and frustrating medication changes with varying side effects, this diet is a fantastic alternative. I will not complain!

This Christmas was our most joyous since the first Christmas after she was born.

—MH

WHEN MEDICATIONS ARE NOT ENOUGH

Seventy percent of children who have a single seizure will never have another. Seventy percent of those who have a second seizure will have their seizures successfully controlled by medication. But if a first medication fails, the chance that a second or third will also be ineffective rises. For about one-fifth of children with epilepsy, currently available medication is either ineffective in controlling seizures or has unacceptable side effects. Even in cases in which seizures are fairly well under control, medication may affect children's alertness and mental clarity, impairing their ability to learn and reach their full potential.

The point at which seizures are deemed out of control, or side effects considered unacceptable, varies from person to person and from family to family. One hundred seizures a day is clearly too many, but are three seizures a month too many? Some children and families consider limiting the seizures to one a week a victory, while others consider one seizure every two months an intolerable state of affairs. Varying degrees of sedation, hyperactivity, and learning disabilities may be acceptable in exchange for seizure control. But what if you could control seizures without side effects? The net result is that many children and their parents look beyond currently available medications for a satisfying solution to seizure treatment.

The ketogenic diet is a rigid, mathematically calculated, doctor-supervised diet. It is high in fat and low in carbohydrate and protein, containing three to five times as much fat as carbohydrate and protein combined. Calories and liquid intake are strictly limited. This diet should not be attempted except under close supervision by a physician. The ketogenic diet improves control of seizures in nearly three-quarters of the children who try it. Twenty to thirty percent may have their seizures completely controlled, and many become free of medication.

Michael is drug-free and seizure-free! He was singing "Jingle Bells" last week, but changed the words to something like this:

> Jingle Bells, I'm a special kid,
> 'Cause I'm on the magic diet.
> Oh, what fun it's gonna be
> To not have seizures anymore!

Isn't that something? We laughed so hard, we cried. Like so many Americans, my faith lay in drugs or surgery. . . . My feelings now cannot be adequately expressed. The meals do take time to prepare, and there are other difficult things to get through, but it's working! IT'S WORKING! Michael is a different child being off the drugs. More alert, more physical, more talkative (boy, is he!). More everything. I feel we now have a whole child. All because of a diet.

I would not wish this diet on my worst enemy, but I would wish it on every child with uncontrolled seizures. It could be the beginning of a whole new life.

—EH

BURNING FAT

The ketogenic diet simulates the metabolism of a fasting body. Since biblical times, fasting has been recognized as a means of controlling seizures. But fasting as a treatment for seizures has one major drawback. Namely, people cannot fast indefinitely because they would starve to death! Also, even if their seizures were controlled by fasting, their seizures would return when they resumed a normal diet.

As a fasting body burns its own fat for energy, so a person on the ketogenic diet derives energy principally by burning fat rather than from the more common energy source, carbohydrate. As the water content of a fasting body is lower than normal, so the ketogenic diet limits liquid intake and lowers the water content of the body. But unlike fasting, the ketogenic diet allows a person to maintain this fat-burning, partially dehydrated metabolism over an extended period of time.

> I call it the "voodoo diet."
>
> My son remembers when he was on the medication. He calls it "when I was bad" or "when I couldn't control myself." He used to rock back and forth, flip the light switch fifty times, make loud noises, bite himself, bite other people, put his hand in a flame, you name it. His seizures were fairly well controlled; he was only having maybe one a month or every six weeks. His doctor said "This kid's seizures are pretty much under control on the medicine. What more do you want?" What I wanted was for my boy to get his old, sweet personality back.
>
> He has had no seizures or medication for a year and a half on the diet. He likes himself now. He is content with who he is. I can hardly believe it. Anyone who sees him can hardly believe he is the same kid. I am certainly glad that I tried this diet, despite the fact that it ties you to the house and it ties you to the meals. I hate the diet. I mean, the minute it's over I'm going to bomb my food scale. But it has helped my son so immensely that I can't hate it too much.
>
> —CC

SAMPLE MEAL PLANS

The ketogenic diet presented in this book is based on the protocol devised by Dr. Samuel Livingston, who was director of the Pediatric Seizure Clinic at the Johns Hopkins Hospital from 1934 to 1971. The most substantial change since that time has been an increased availability of information on nutrition and food content. As a result, we can include a much wider variety of foods in the diet. This makes the diet more flexible and palatable than it was in Dr. Livingston's era. Following is an example of what a couple of days' meal plans might look like for a child on the diet:

BREAKFAST

Scrambled eggs with butter

Diluted cream

Orange juice

LUNCH

Spaghetti squash with butter
and Parmesan cheese

Lettuce leaf with mayonnaise

Orange diet soda mixed with
whipped cream

DINNER

Hot dog slices with catsup

Asparagus with butter

Chopped lettuce with mayonnaise

Vanilla cream popsicle

BREAKFAST

Bacon

Scrambled egg with butter

Melon slices

Vanilla cream shake

LUNCH

Tuna with mayonnaise

Celery and cucumber sticks

Sugarless Jell-O with whipped
cream

DINNER

Broiled chicken breast

Chopped lettuce with mayonnaise

Cinnamon apple slice with butter
topped with vanilla ice cream

By identifying the four main food groups of the diet—protein, fruit or vegetable, fat, and cream—in each of these menus, you can begin to understand how the diet is constructed. This will be explained in greater detail later in the book.

The ketogenic diet must be calculated with precision, prepared meticulously using a gram scale, and followed rigidly. To optimize the chance of success, the diet must be undertaken with the supervision of a dietitian trained in its use and a physician familiar with its many quirks. Success requires the commitment, determination, and faith of the entire family.

A ONE-MONTH TRIAL

We ask families to try the ketogenic diet initially for one month. This takes discipline and willpower. It starts with an initiation and training period of several days in the hospital. Then we ask parents and children to stick with the diet for a month in the face of all the food temptations and other difficulties that come along in daily life. In a single month we can usually ascertain if the diet is likely to be effective for a child. If the diet is working or shows potential to be effective, most families find that it is well worth the time, trouble, and effort to stick with the diet over a two- to three-year period. If it is not working after a month, the family can go back to trying to control the seizures through medication.

WHO IS A CANDIDATE FOR THE DIET?

The ketogenic diet has classically been used as a last resort, when seizures remain incapacitating despite the use of two or three medications in combination, medications that may have been shuffled and adjusted over a period of months or even years. Since the diet is so dramatically effective in this extreme population, perhaps it should be used earlier in the course of a child's difficult-to-control epilepsy, rather than merely as a last resort. Perhaps children should be considered as candidates for the diet as soon as a second medication fails to control their seizures. At present, there is little experience in adolescents, and even less in adults. We only recommend the diet in children with difficult-to-control seizures occurring several times each week

> When your child is a zombie, when he sleeps practically the whole day and his eyes are glazed over, the whole family kind of feels sick. If you can get improvement with the diet, and the child starts being brighter and more responsive, the whole family feels better and breathes a sigh of relief. Even though weighing all the child's food and being tied down to strict meal plans is far from easy, it's worth it if you can improve the quality of life of your whole family.
>
> —LF

SEIZURE TYPES AND STRUCTURAL DISORDERS

The ketogenic diet is particularly effective in controlling childhood myoclonic, absence, and atonic (drop) seizures, which are particularly difficult to control with standard medication. The diet also helps some patients with generalized tonic-clonic (grand mal) seizures, and even the multifocal seizures of the Lennox-Gastaut syndrome.

The ketogenic diet may be tried on children with any type of seizure; unlike anticonvulsant medication, it does not appear to have any adverse side effects. Even children with structural brain disorders such as microcephaly, hypoxic brain damage, prior strokes, and developmental abnormalities have had success with the diet. If a child has noticeably fewer seizures when sick or unable to eat, this may indicate potential for that child's success on the diet.

FIGURE 1.   SEIZURE TYPES experienced by a sample of fifteen patients initiated on the ketogenic diet at the Johns Hopkins Pediatric Epilepsy Center during the first half of 1994. Many children have more than one seizure type.

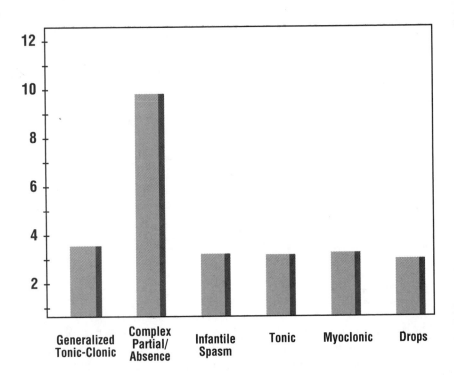

AGE

The ketogenic diet is most often prescribed for children over one year of age. Children under the age of one year have trouble becoming ketotic and maintaining ketosis. They are also prone to hypoglycemia. Therefore, the diet is not often advised for children under one year old. Traditionally the diet was rarely used in school-age children since it was believed that their dietary habits were too ingrained and that food temptations for children outside the home would be too great. An older child who already goes to school and loves McDonald's may find the diet more difficult than a very young child who has not yet formed strong eating habits. A child whose friends are eating pizza and cookies in the school cafeteria will be more tempted to cheat than one who spends all day with a parent. But in their determination to defeat their seizure disorders, older children can often summon up the willpower to resist temptation. As long as it controls their seizures, many children wouldn't give up their ketogenic meals for anything. The strength and determination of many of these children amazes their parents and teachers.

> At first we didn't go out, even to my parents'. I was afraid of temptation, of making my son sad for what he couldn't have. But he missed the socializing. He said, "How come we never go out anymore?" I told him, "You couldn't order anything on the menu anyway." He said, "I could get ice for my ginger ale!" Now we go to a restaurant and take his meal with us. He tells the waitress, "I'm on a special diet so just bring me ice, please."
>
> —CC

The ketogenic diet may therefore be recommended for older children provided that they and their families are highly motivated. In our experience, even determined adolescents have completed the diet successfully. After infancy, motivation is more important than age in determining the potential success of the diet. Few adults have been tried on the diet. It has been said that adults have difficulty maintaining ketosis, but to our knowledge this has not been studied in depth.

> Nobody thought this child was going to stay on this diet. I am really amazed he has stuck to it as well as he has. He really fooled me. He used to snack constantly in front of the television. But by the time Brian started the diet, he was ready for it. He was really embarrassed by his seizures, ready to try anything. Now he has no seizures and he wants to start going to school dances. I'm so proud of him. I can't believe it.
>
> —FD

INTELLIGENCE

The level of a child's intelligence is not a criterion for selecting appropriate candidates for the diet. Some of our most dramatic successes have occurred in profoundly handicapped children. Other successes have occurred in children with normal intelligence.

NEW APPROACHES

It is our intention throughout this book to make the diet available to the many families whose children are severely and profoundly handicapped by seizures or by the adverse side effects of current medications. Sometimes the ketogenic diet will free these children from both seizures and medications. When the diet is most effective, the children may after a time be "cured," in the sense that the diet may be slowly withdrawn and the children return to a normal diet while remaining seizure-free without medication.

We hope that future researchers, dietitians, epileptologists, neuroscientists, and parents will see for themselves that this diet can work almost miraculously, allowing children plagued by a myriad of seizures

FIGURE 2. AGE IN YEARS of patients initiated on the ketogenic diet at the Johns Hopkins Pediatric Epilepsy Center from 1990 to 1994.

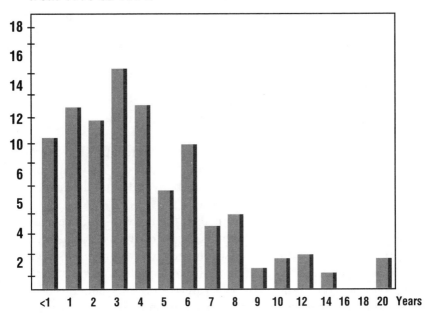

to become seizure-free, and allowing children incapacitated by medications the freedom to develop to their full potential. Seeing this with their own eyes, perhaps members of the medical community will begin to use modern technology to understand the mechanisms involved. Perhaps this will lead to the discovery of new approaches to seizure control—and seizure cure.

When a parent calls up and tells me a child hasn't had seizures in six months, that's the most wonderful news in the world.

—MK

How the Diet Works

When parents come into the hospital with their children to initiate the diet, we explain to them that the body burns three types of fuel to produce energy. These fuel types are:

- CARBOHYDRATES: Starches, sugars, breads, cereal grains, fruits, vegetables.
- FATS: Butter, margarine, oil, mayonnaise.
- PROTEINS: Meat, fish, poultry, cheese, eggs, milk.

Carbohydrates comprise about 50 to 60 percent of the average American's daily caloric intake. They are the least expensive and most efficient source of food energy. When carbohydrates are digested, the body converts them to glucose.

Glucose is the fuel source burned by the body to produce energy under normal circumstances. When its supply of glucose is limited, the body first burns adipose (fatty) tissue for energy. If caloric needs are not met by body fat, the body then draws from its protein stores (muscle), compromising good health. The body cannot store large amounts of glucose; it maintains only about a twenty-four-hour supply. Fasting for twenty-four hours depletes body glucose. Once glucose is depleted, as during fasting, the body automatically draws on its other energy source—stored body fat.

In the absence of glucose, fat is not burned completely, but leaves a residue of "soot" or "ash" in the form of ketone bodies (acetone and aceto-acetic acid). These ketone bodies build up in the blood. The excess is cleaned out by the kidneys and excreted in the urine.

The ketogenic diet deliberately maintains this buildup of ketone bodies in the blood by forcing the body to burn fat, instead of glucose, as its primary source of energy. When ketone bodies are large enough, as indicated by a simple urine test, it is said that the body is "ketotic" (pronounced key-tah´-tic) or in a state of "ketosis." Ketosis is also evidenced by a fruity, sweet odor to the breath.

Fat energy is the basis of the ketogenic diet. In the presence of large levels of ketone bodies, seizures are frequently controlled.

Unfortunately, we do not yet know precisely why the diet works. We will tell you what we do know in Chapter 3.

Answers to Common Questions

1. My child loves pizza and ice cream. Eating is an important part of our family life. How could we ever go on the diet successfully?

If you are creative, you can find a way to adapt and still follow the diet. Pizza? Try a grilled tomato or eggplant slice topped with cheese—this becomes a ketogenic pizza. Ice cream? No problem! The cream in the diet can be frozen into scoops or popsicles, flavored with allowed sweeteners and baking chocolate, vanilla, or strawberries. The kind of pizza or ice cream your child is accustomed to having may seem unimportant when a "magic diet" helps to get rid of seizures!

Your child can go on the diet successfully because both of you want to cure the seizures. Much, perhaps most, of the diet's success will depend on your positive attitude and persuasiveness as a parent. If a parent does not have a positive attitude, the child will not cooperate and the diet will not work.

2. Won't my child gain weight on all that fatty food?

On this diet the amount of food is carefully calculated so that your child will eat all the calories and protein needed for good health, but not so many that weight is gained. The fat content of the food has no bearing on weight as long as overall calories are strictly limited. Although restricting calories is important for achieving seizure control, calories will be adjusted up or down if abnormal weight gain or loss occurs. It is normal for weight gain to accompany growth in height, but even this growth may be slowed while your child is on the diet. Height and weight will catch up when your child returns to a normal diet.

3. Suppose my daughter eats a piece of toast. Will she go out of ketosis? Will I have to start over?

Yes, she may go out of ketosis, but you will not have to start over. You may, however, need to bring your child back into ketosis by skipping a meal or two until ketones in the urine reach the four-plus level, then start meals again as usual. If a mistake like this causes a breakthrough seizure, it will not spoil the long-term effects of the diet. Even so, loss of ketosis should be kept to a minimum.

4. My child was seizure-free on the diet for three weeks but had a seizure yesterday. Why?

The most common cause of a breakthrough seizure in a child who has been well controlled on the diet is eating food that is not part of the meal plans. Family members and others often do not understand the need for strict compliance, and slip food to the child thinking they are being nice. Incorrect preparation methods, such as purchasing a new commercial food product not calculated into a meal plan, can also lead to problems, as can medications containing glucose or carbohydrates. Illness might also cause breakthrough seizures in some children. If a breakthrough seizure occurs in a child who has been well controlled on the diet, it is almost always due to an aberration or mistake, and seizure control can almost always be reestablished.

5. If my child has a seizure after being well controlled for three weeks on the diet, what should I do?

First, check to see if your child ate something extra. Could a friend have offered a spare cookie? Might Grandma have slipped in a chocolate? Is the dog's food sealed tightly? Is the toothpaste missing? Have any new or different medicines or vitamin supplements been taken? Even a spoonful of regular cough syrup or sugarless foods containing sugar substitutes with carbohydrate, such as mannitol, sorbitol, polydextrose, or maltodextrin, can cause breakthrough seizures.

Next, review your preparation methods. Did you do anything different? Did you weigh vegetables raw that should have been cooked? Buy a new brand of sausage? Measuring oil by volume instead of by weight could be a problem if you are using a large amount of oil. All food should be measured on a gram scale.

Is your child gaining weight? Weight gain is one sign that the diet is not being properly calculated or prepared. If the diet is providing more calories than your child's body needs to maintain itself, seizures may continue or recur. In such a case, the calorie count may need to be reduced slightly. Since every child's situation is different, you will need to do some sleuthing to solve the problem. Your doctor or dietitian may also be able to isolate the possible cause of seizures by listening to you and carefully reviewing your child's diet.

If your child was previously having frequent seizures and then was seizure-free for several weeks on the diet, the diet is likely to be effective despite the breakthrough seizures—it just needs fine-tuning.

6. I am doing everything my doctor told me but my child's seizures are continuing. What more can I do?

Go over the diet and your home circumstances with a fine-tooth comb with your dietitian to be sure there are no mistakes in preparation or anyone giving unplanned food. Perhaps better seizure control could be achieved with fewer calories. Changing to a more restrictive 4.5:1 ratio of fat to protein plus carbohydrate for a few months may help. In some cases, a 5:1 ketogenic ratio is needed. Some children on the ketogenic diet will continue to have some seizures. The goal of the diet is to reduce the number and intensity of seizures as much as you can; complete control is not always possible. In the end it is up to you to decide whether the diet's rigor is worth the level of seizure control and freedom from medications that it provides your child. Some children's seizures do not respond or do not respond sufficiently well to continue the diet.

7. Is the ketogenic diet nutritionally complete?

The ketogenic diet is nutritionally complete when proper supplements are taken. Multivitamins and calcium must be given as dietary supplements in sugar-free form. Some people ask whether carnitine should be added to the diet. We have conducted the diet for decades without carnitine, and no data indicate that it is necessary or useful as a supplement. Since carnitine is expensive, we do not use it or any supplements other than sugar-free multivitamins and calcium. Some nutritionists have also claimed that the diet is deficient in trace minerals such as zinc and selenium. All we can say is that we have treated scores of children without any evidence of adverse effects from the absence of micronutrients.

8. What can my child eat at school?

Your dietitian will help you plan meals that can easily be transported to school. Tuna, egg, or chicken salads are particularly easy to carry in Tupperware containers. Warm or chilled food can be carried in a small cooler or insulated bag, or wrapped in foil. Your child will have to learn to tell the teacher and classmates "No, thanks!" when snacks are distributed to the class. For occasions such as birthday parties, you can send your child to school with a container of special cheesecake or frozen eggnog (see Chapter 4) that can be eaten when the other kids eat their cake. It is remarkable how even young children of four or five years can learn to refuse treats, saying, "I'm a special kid on a special diet."

9. Can we go to a restaurant or on a day's outing while my child is on the diet?

With imagination, planning, and persistence, you and your child can go anywhere on the diet. On short trips, you can take one or several pre-prepared meals along in a cooler or Thermos. Some families ask to have a pre-prepared meal heated in a restaurant's microwave. Additionally, before you leave the hospital your dietitian will calculate an eggnog recipe that can be used as an easy meal replacement if you are in transit at mealtime (see Chapter 4).

10. Can we go on family trips?

You may go on longer trips if all the ingredients of your child's diet are under your control. You can stay in a hotel or motel with a kitchenette, for instance. In a pinch, you can order plain broiled meat or chicken, steamed vegetables or fresh fruit, butter, and heavy whipping cream at a restaurant, and weigh portions on your scale when the food arrives. Remember, though, that tiny bits of extra foods such as catsup, dill pickle, or lemon juice can upset your child's ketosis if they are not calculated into the meal. For greater detail on how to preserve your mobility while on the diet, see Chapter 7.

11. The amounts of food allowed in the diet are so small—won't my child feel hungry?

Ketosis suppresses appetite, so children on the diet are not usually as hungry as other children. The diet is hypocaloric, providing only about three-quarters of the calories that would normally be recommended for a child's height and weight. However, ketosis and the concentration of fat in the diet help to create a full feeling in the stomach despite the small quantity of food. Some children feel hungry for the first week or two of the diet, but their stomachs usually adjust with time.

12. What if my child refuses to eat all the food in a meal?

Because of the small quantity, children usually need to eat all of the food on the diet in order to feel full. If your child does refuse food, however, you must use your powers of persuasion and try to create a menu that might be more acceptable for the next meal. The key to success is to be creative, not rigid, within the bounds of the diet. Ultimately, to provide proper nutrition and maintain ketosis, all of the food in a meal must be consumed at one time—it may not be saved until the next meal or eaten between meals. If ketosis is not maintained, the diet will not work.

13. My daughter is doing so well on the diet. She has had no seizures. But there is a lot of flu going around and she vomited all last evening. This afternoon her ketones are low. Why? What should I do?

The low ketones may well be due to the infection and the alterations in her metabolism caused by her illness. Since she has been doing so well on the diet and is bright and alert, you should probably do nothing. She will most likely be back to eating by the evening or the next day. In the meantime, you should make sure she gets enough liquid to stay hydrated. You might also try offering eggnog; since every sip is balanced in terms of its ketogenic ratio, it does not matter if your child only drinks a little bit.

If dehydration becomes a real problem, it may be necessary to give some Pedialyte (a chemically balanced fluid available at the drugstore). Pedialyte contains about twenty-three grams of carbohydrate per 1,000 cc. When the child is not eating any food, the carbohydrate in Pedialyte often is no greater than the combined protein and carbohydrate allotment in the diet, so Pedialyte often does not upset ketosis. In case of severe dehydration, it may be necessary to get an intravenous saline solution at the hospital. Intravenous dextrose should not be used because it will upset ketosis.

14. What if my daughter has a seizure while she is sick with the flu?

Illness may sometimes cause a transient drop in ketone levels. If your daughter starts to have seizures during an illness, following recovery you can put her on a fast for one to three meals until she goes back into ketosis, and then restart the diet, perhaps at half quantity for a few meals. The effectiveness of the diet is only partly represented by large ketones in the urine. Some children have seizures even while their urinary ketones remain high, while others may do well despite a transient drop in ketones. The most important measure is how well the child is doing.

15. My son got bronchitis and his doctor prescribed an antibiotic. How do I know if this will affect the diet?

When on the diet all medicines and pharmaceuticals, from toothpaste to cough syrup to vitamins to prescription medicine, must be free of all sugar and carbohydrate whenever possible. Some common forms of sugar and carbohydrate to watch out for on labels are: glucose, sucrose, fructose, dextrose, sorbitol, and mannitol. Medication in chewable or tablet form often contains some carbohydrate to bind the tablet together, and sweet-tasting elixirs or syrups often contain sugar. Ask your doctor to prescribe needed medications in sugar-free and carbohydrate-free forms. If you have questions, the best source of information is your pharmacist. In fact, a pharmacist is often an important part of the ketogenic diet team, helping parents through their child's illnesses throughout the duration of the diet. If your pharmacist cannot help, go directly to the manufacturer. Formulas often change; read labels carefully and don't take anything for granted. In an emergency, or if it is not possible to find a sugar-free formula, take care of your child's health first. (See Appendix A on medications for more detail.)

16. The ketogenic diet is making my child constipated. How do I keep this from being a problem?

If constipation is a problem, try to use meal plans that contain as much fiber as possible. You are allowed to use two lettuce leaves, or about one-half cup of chopped lettuce, per day as a "free" food, and you can use calculated mayonnaise as dressing. Using more Group A vegetables can also help, since you can serve twice as many of these as of Group B vegetables. Try cutting out meal plans with catsup, chocolate, or other carbohydrate-based flavorings that take away from the quantity of fiber-rich vegetables your child can eat. In extreme cases, you can use a stool softener such as Colace or a gentle laxative such as Milk of Magnesia, diluted Baby Fleet enemas, or other children's rectal suppositories. One mother used a diluted enema regularly every other day, pouring out two-thirds of the dosage so the long-term use would not hurt her son's bowels. MCT oil, in small amounts, may be calculated into the diet to relieve constipation. Cal-Mag may also be useful. (For more on constipation see Chapter 6.)

17. Is it possible for a child to become too ketotic?

Yes. The level of ketone bodies may become unusually high and a child may experience shallow, panting breathing, but this is rare. If this happens, give the child a sip of orange juice or a cracker to bring the ketone levels back in the normal high ketone range. If it becomes a recurring problem, the dietitian should try reducing the child's ketogenic ratio to 3:1.

THREE

A Medical Overview of the Ketogenic Diet: Its History, Background, and Use

Some say the ketogenic diet sounds like a form of witchcraft. Thirty grams cream, twelve grams meat, eighteen grams butter—the recipe begins to resemble that of Shakespeare's old witches concocting their brew. There is mystery to it. We do not understand how or why the ketogenic diet works. But we do know that it *does* work, and we have known this for seventy years. We know that:

- The diet will completely control epilepsy in one-third of the children whose seizures are otherwise uncontrollable.
- In half of the remaining children, the diet will either markedly decrease the frequency of seizures or enable medications to be reduced.
- Many children whose seizures are completely controlled can return to a normal diet in two to three years and remain seizure-free without medication. They have either been cured of epilepsy or have recovered from their previously uncontrollable epilepsy. Permanent control often begins within days of diet initiation.

FIGURE 3. SEIZURE FREQUENCY with ketogenic diet initiation. After one month, two of seven patients were seizure-free. One was down to one brief episode per day. One child was taken off the diet. Three others, having markedly decreased seizure activity, elected to continue to work with the diet.

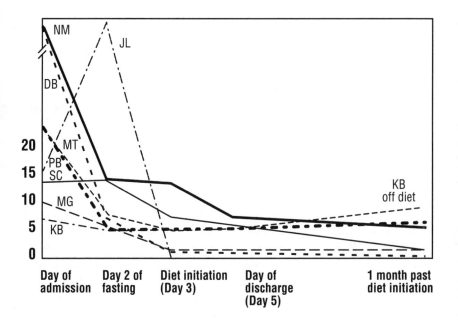

In this era of increasingly high-tech medicine, the ketogenic diet is very low-tech. Even so, we cannot yet articulate a cogent theory of its mechanism of action. On the other hand, we do not understand much about epilepsy either. Little is known about the mechanisms by which seizures spread throughout the brain. We do not understand why seizures occur at one moment but not at another, or why one child's seizure threshold is lower than another's. To be truthful, little is known about how the various anticonvulsants work either. If we understand so little about the causes underlying seizures and the mechanisms of the medications commonly used to treat epilepsy, it should not be surprising that we do not understand the mechanisms of their treatment with an old-fashioned diet.

BACKGROUND

Fasting has long been recognized as one approach to seizure control. In the early 1900s, abstinence from food for a few days was found to result in cessation of seizures and improvement in mental function. Unfortunately, fasting is not a feasible long-term solution to the problems of epilepsy. Fasting, while temporarily effective, causes no permanent resolution of seizures, as it obviously cannot be maintained indefinitely.

There are a number of stories about how the ketogenic diet was developed out of an interest in fasting, and how it came to be utilized for treatment of epilepsy. One story involves Johns Hopkins, so we will tell it first, although we have been unable to verify fully the authenticity of every detail.

Dr. W.G. Lennox, one of the pioneers of modern epilepsy research, recounts in his book *Epilepsy and Related Disorders* the story of a New York corporate lawyer whose son, HTH, had uncontrollable daily seizures. This was during the early 1920s, when phenobarbital and bromides were the principal anticonvulsant medications available, and these were ineffective in controlling HTH's frequent seizures. In desperation, the family turned to Hugh Conklin, an osteopathic practitioner in Battle Creek, Michigan. Conklin was a disciple of Bernard McFadden, a physical cultist who believed in managing illness with prayer and a water diet that involved starvation for three to four weeks. Participation in this prayer and fasting improved the child's seizures dramatically. Prayer alone was ineffective, and prolonged fasting was impractical, so the father searched for an alternative solution.

This took place early in the era of nutritional research in children when many of the giants of pediatric nutrition—Drs. Howland, Blackfan, and Gamble among them—were beginning their classic studies of the body's chemical changes during diarrhea and fasting at the recently founded Harriet Lane Laboratories at the Johns Hopkins Hospital in Baltimore. Dr. John Howland, who in 1912 had become the first full-time head of the Department of Pediatrics at Johns Hopkins, the first such appointment in America, had established one of the first clinical laboratories capable of studying disease using the techniques of quantitative chemistry. Dr. Howland, an uncle of HTH, enlisted the aid of his laboratory colleagues in an attempt to understand how fasting controlled epilepsy and how the fasting state and its benefits could be maintained. By 1919, Dr. Howland had developed a deep interest in the treatment of epilepsy by what he called "the ketosis of starvation." Dr. James Gamble, soon to become one of the great figures in the field of pediatric fluid and electrolyte balance, joined this research effort when he returned from World War I.

During fasting, they discovered, in addition to ketosis from the incomplete burning of carbohydrates and the accompanying acidosis, a large amount of uric acid is excreted in the urine. If a fast was broken by the ingestion of sugars, carbohydrates, or protein, this urinary uric

FIGURE 4. DAILY NUMBER of minor attacks with reference to prefasting number. Ketosis developed after two or three days. From Lennox and Cobb (1928).

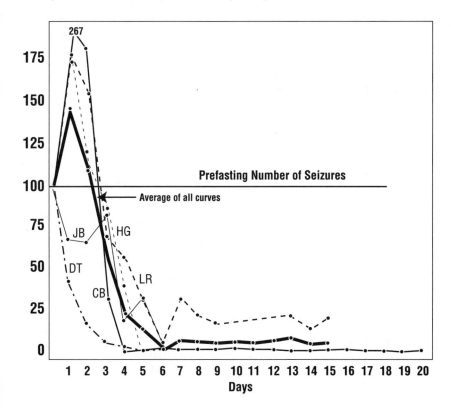

acid output ceased. If a fast was broken with 40 percent fat, however, uric acid excretion continued. Following this discovery, a diet was devised which would closely mimic the body's reaction to fasting—causing acidosis, ketosis, and increased blood and urine levels of uric acid. Although it is now known that uric acid is the product of protein breakdown by the body, and that carbohydrate has a protein-sparing effect that decreases uric acid production, at the time it was believed that an increase in blood levels of uric acid was important in the control of seizures.

Meanwhile, at the Mayo Clinic in Minnesota, Dr. R.M. Wilder suggested in 1921 that a diet of high fat and low carbohydrate could reproduce the ketosis and acidosis of starvation and be maintained far longer than fasting. The diet Dr. Wilder devised, which provided the minimal amount of protein required for growth and most of its calories as fat, was termed the "ketogenic diet."*

Whether the use of this diet and its fine-tuning were the results of Wilder's efforts at the Mayo Clinic or those of Howland and Gamble at Hopkins, or of further efforts by Lennox and a Harvard group, is of little importance. The beneficial results of this ketogenic diet were soon reported by physicians from the Mayo Clinic (Wilder 1921, Peterman 1923), Harvard (Lennox 1928), and many other centers.

In the 1960s, Lennox summarized many prior studies when he wrote, "probably one-third of the children who maintain an adequate ketogenic diet for a prolonged period become seizure-free and another one-third

---

* The ketogenic diet as developed by Wilder and a fellow diabetologist at the Mayo Clinic is based on the concept that some foods are more likely to increase the body's production of ketone bodies, while others are "anti-ketogenic." Any glucose will exert an anti-ketogenic effect because it is completely burned by the body. A small portion of ingested fat (1 part of 10), a significant part of protein (more than half), and all carbohydrates are broken down to glucose and are anti-ketogenic. This has been expressed in the formula:

$$\frac{\text{Ketogenic}}{\text{Anti-Ketogenic}} = \frac{K}{AK} = \frac{0.9 \text{ Fat} + 0.46 \text{ Protein}}{1.0 \text{ Carbohydrate} + 0.1 \text{ Fat} + 0.58 \text{ Protein}}$$

The ketogenic/anti–ketogenic ratio of food in a diet must be at least 1.5:1 to produce noticeably elevated levels of ketone bodies in the blood and urine. Seizure control is best when the ratio is at least 3:1. Calories must be limited to maintain ketosis.

are much improved." In a 1992 study of the ketogenic diet in children whose seizures remain uncontrolled despite modern medicine, we found that 30 percent achieved complete control of their seizures and an additional 38 percent had marked improvement in seizure control. In spite of the discovery of the many new and effective anticonvulsants that now successfully control seizures in almost 80 percent of children with epilepsy, the success rates of the ketogenic diet in children with uncontrollable seizures today are very similar to those reported beginning in the 1920s.

THEORETICAL BASIS OF THE KETOGENIC DIET

Aside from the short answer "we don't really know," the longer answer to the question of how the ketogenic diet functions is that there may be a combination of factors at work:

- KETONE BODIES come in many chemical forms and are the result of the incomplete burning of fats in the body. Ketone bodies have a sedative effect and an appetite-suppressing effect. Some popular weight-reduction diets with very low calorie levels and low carbohydrates produce ketosis. The appetite-suppressing effect of ketosis explains why these diets can be followed without the dieter's feeling too hungry. Ketone bodies also have an anticonvulsant effect. However, ketones by themselves do not adequately explain the effectiveness of the ketogenic diet. For example, when a child whose seizures are well controlled on the diet eats a cookie, seizures may occur even if urinary ketones are not clearly affected. While their concentration in the blood is perhaps more important, we measure ketones in the urine for convenience. If there are no ketones in the urine, the diet is not going to work. Ketones in the blood and in the urine are necessary for the diet to be effective, but the presence of ketones alone is not sufficient.
- ACIDOSIS means an increased amount of acid in the blood. Ketone bodies are acids and therefore cause acidosis. There are several other chemical mechanisms by which the human body produces acidosis, and many ways in which the body compensates for ketones to maintain a normal pH balance. Acidosis influences the threshold for seizures. This is why the ingestion of acids or

acid-forming salts, or breathing a mixture high in carbon dioxide, can reduce seizures temporarily, just as hyperventilating, which reduces acidosis, can bring out seizures. Acidosis may be one of the participants facilitating seizure control in the ketogenic diet, but since the body quickly compensates for the acidosis to readjust its pH balance, acidosis cannot be the major determinant of the diet's success.

- DEHYDRATION was part of the original water diet used by McFadden that ultimately led to the development of the ketogenic diet. While fluids are traditionally limited during the diet, the role, if any, of dehydration in seizure control is unclear. It is known that administering excess water can provoke seizures, probably due to acute dilution of the body's sodium level. Indeed, this was one of the methods used by physicians to provoke seizures for observation. However, this in no way indicates that dehydration would prevent seizures by raising the body's sodium level. Normal kidneys do an excellent job of maintaining the body's chemical balance. Another misconception about fluid intake is that fluid dilutes the ketones, thereby negating the effects of the ketogenic diet. Increased water intake certainly results in urine that is more dilute. If the body's production and excretion of ketones is constant, the concentration of ketones in the urine (and therefore the strength of the urinary ketone test) will depend on the child's water intake. This does not, however, necessarily reflect the level of ketones in the blood and brain, which may be higher.

None of the individual mechanisms discussed here will in isolation lead to seizure control, since the body can compensate for each of them. Acidosis corrects itself in one to two weeks, and the pH of the blood will then remain normal throughout the remainder of the diet. Changes in the water and electrolyte content of the brain are rapidly compensated for by the rest of the body.

The real effectiveness of the diet probably lies in other influences on metabolism. For example, while the brains of infants, children, and adults burns glucose almost exclusively, the fetus and newborn are able to exist on the metabolism of fats. Does the ketogenic diet enable the brain to revert to a more primitive form of metabolism? Is the reason that the ketogenic diet is more effective in children than in adults based on the younger brain's capability to metabolize fats? There is also some suggestion that a diet high in certain fats, particularly B-hydroxybuter-ate, may alter the chemistry of brain cell membranes and thereby the sensitivity of certain transmitter sites. Clearly, more research is needed to explore the mechanisms by which the ketogenic diet achieves its dramatic results.

THE NEED FOR RESEARCH

In the early 1960s, Dr. H. Houston Merritt, co-discoverer of Dilantin and then director of the Neurologic Institute at the Columbia Presbyterian Medical Center in New York, told his residents that the discovery of Dilantin was a major setback to the understanding of epilepsy. At the time the effectiveness of Dilantin was discovered in the 1930s, many people were investigating brain metabolism in epilepsy and beginning to study the mechanisms by which the ketogenic diet stopped seizures.

Since the discovery of Dilantin, however, efforts have been directed toward finding other drugs that would be equally effective, and no one has gone back to look at the basic mechanisms by which the diet alters the brain's metabolism.

With new imaging technology such as positron emission tomography (PET) and single photon emission computerized tomography (SPECT) scans, and with advancements in magnetic resonance imaging (MRI) spectroscopy, we can now study the human brain in action. With MRI we can study the chemical and metabolic changes that rapidly take place during changing conditions such as seizures. We should begin to study the brain metabolism of individual children who are having frequent seizures. We can conduct studies in the same child under conditions of starvation and during initiation of the ketogenic diet. We could analyze acute changes in metabolism and evaluate longer-term changes in brain energy metabolism with continuation of the diet.

We could use studies of children for whom the diet is unsuccessful as controls to compare with those in whom the diet stops seizures. We can even use the same child as his or her own control by giving a child whose seizures are well controlled on the diet a small dose of glucose and then studying any alterations in brain metabolism that take place subsequently. Through studies such as these, and others that physicians will conceive, we can hope to improve understanding in the future of why and through what mechanisms the ketogenic diet works.

Use of the Ketogenic Diet—A Physician's View

> My child neurologist never even mentioned the ketogenic
> diet. When I read about it in *Seizures and Epilepsy in
> Childhood**, I asked my doctor and he said that it didn't
> work. How is it that a child neurologist doesn't know about
> this diet?
>
> —TP

The diet fell into disuse during the 1940s and 1950s for several reasons. Newer anticonvulsant medications became available one after another. It was far easier for parents and for the patients themselves to swallow one or several pills each day than to comply with such a rigorous diet. Compared with new, ever-developing medications, the diet came to seem like too much trouble. There was always hope that the next anticonvulsant pill or combination of medications would help.

The diet is a lot of trouble. No one would dispute that. But if it works—if it works—it becomes not only tolerable, but "amazing," "fantastic," "a miracle," as can be loudly heard from the parents of children for whom it has been successful.

In an era committed to placing hope in newer and newer medications, though, the diet was prescribed less and less frequently. Fewer physicians were trained in its use, so it was ordered even less frequently; thus, fewer dietitians had any experience in calculating and fine-tuning the diet. The ketogenic diet gradually became little more than a vague memory to most of the medical and the dietetic communities. As few people had direct experience with it, the diet was thought to be unpalatable, and many doctors believed that parents and children would not be strong or rigorous enough to comply.

---

*Freeman JM, Vining EPG, and Pillas DJ, *Seizures and Epilepsy in Childhood: A Guide for Parents*. Baltimore: Johns Hopkins University Press, 1990.

The MCT Diet

> We have already been on the ketogenic diet once. We used that MCT oil stuff, and it was awful. Our daughter had terrible diarrhea and the seizures didn't improve, so we stopped after two weeks. Why would you suggest that we consider trying it again?
>
> —TP

In the belief that the ketogenic diet was an effective form of therapy and that more families would try—and benefit from—a ketogenic diet if it were formulated with foods more closely approximating a normal diet, Dr. Peter Huttenlocher of the University of Chicago and his colleagues devised a diet that they believed would be more palatable than the "classical" ketogenic diet, and which would therefore foster compliance, while maintaining ketosis. They called their formulation the MCT diet, replacing the long-chain fats of the classical ketogenic diet with medium-chain triglycerides (MCT), which come as an odorless, colorless, tasteless oil. MCTs contain fatty acids with shorter molecular chain lengths than the long-chain triglycerides found in cream, butter, and most other dietary fats.

An MCT diet with calories at 100 percent of RDA levels, and with more carbohydrates and protein, will produce the same ketosis as a classical diet with calories at 75 percent of RDA levels. MCT oil can thus be said to be more ketogenic than other dietary fats. Because the diet is more ketogenic, a child on the MCT diet can eat a wider variety of anti-ketogenic foods, such as larger portions of fruit and vegetables and even a small amount of bread and other starches. Fluids are not restricted on this diet.

The MCT diet, like the classical ketogenic diet, is initiated after a brief fast and usually shows results within several days of its inception. Children must stick with it rigidly, as with the classical ketogenic diet, and if the MCT diet works, children similarly stay on it for about two years.

Although the MCT diet has been reported to be equally as effective as the classical ketogenic diet, this has not been our experience at Johns Hopkins. We have found that the MCT diet is too high in calories (thus providing inferior seizure control) and is not more palatable than the classical diet. In fact, our experience indicates that ingestion of the MCT oil is often accompanied by abdominal cramps, severe and persistent diarrhea, or by nausea and vomiting. If children cannot hold it down, it cannot be effective.

A comparison of the classical ketogenic diet with the MCT diet and a modified ketogenic diet (Schwartz et al.) found all three to be equally effective in achieving seizure control. Compliance and palatability, however, were found to be better with the classical ketogenic diet.

Many parents tell us that their child has already been on the ketogenic diet without success. On further questioning, this prior diet usually turns out to have been the MCT diet. We have found some children who continued to have seizures despite tolerating the MCT diet, but who subsequently responded well to the classical ketogenic diet. We have also seen many children and families who could not tolerate the MCT diet but who did well on the classical ketogenic diet. In other words, we at Hopkins have found that a little imagination applied to the classical ketogenic diet is more effective with regard to palatability than is Huttenlocher's MCT formulation.

Some parents or physicians may want to try the MCT diet for children, perhaps with the thought of providing a higher volume of food. If the child does not have trouble with the oil, and if the seizures are completely controlled, some families appreciate the additional anti-ketogenic calories that the MCT diet affords. If the MCT diet does not work, or if it is not tolerated, we recommend trying the classical ketogenic diet.

THE KETOGENIC DIET TODAY

These days, information on the nutritional content of almost all food is readily available. Numerous books provide nutritional information for a wide variety of foods. Information on processed foods, if not shown on the label, is available from the manufacturer upon request. The importance of nutrition is appreciated more than ever, as demonstrated in nutrition-based treatment of high cholesterol, diabetes, and renal or heart disease. At the same time, research has shown that all the modern medication and technology currently available cannot control some 20 percent of children with epilepsy.

Even now, of course, the diet is a lot of work on the part of the parents as well as the dietitians, especially in the first weeks. It requires persistence, care, and faith on the part of the whole team: the physician and the dietitian as well as the parents. The history of the diet reveals that disuse has engendered mistrust. But this, too, may pass. The medical community can now look back and judge the history of anticonvulsant medications—their efficacy and side effects—and compare this to the efficacy of the ketogenic diet. With the knowledge embodied in this book and the convenience of computer calculations, we hope that physicians and dietitians will regain a familiarity with the benefits of the ketogenic diet and begin to use it more frequently.

Sample Meal Plans

A child on the ketogenic diet can eat a wide range of food—perhaps not exactly the same food eaten prior to the diet, but pretty satisfying nevertheless. The food is especially gratifying if accompanied by few or no seizures!

> As often as possible, Michael has at least one thing that we are having. If I am making pork chops for us, I cook him one. If we are having tuna fish sandwiches, he has tuna fish with mayonnaise wrapped in a leaf of lettuce. . . . At least one part of his meal [is] the same as ours. I think this helps the child to accept the diet.
>
> —EH

For each child who embarks on the ketogenic diet a set of individually tailored meal plans should be calculated after discussing food preferences and family eating habits with the child's parents. We use a nutrition history form at Johns Hopkins to learn about a child's habits, routines, likes, and dislikes, so that meal plans can be calculated to resemble the family's normal meals as closely as possible. If there is time, we send this form to parents prior to admission. Otherwise we ask parents to fill it out when they arrive at the hospital to initiate the diet. The nutrition history form is reproduced in Chapter 5.

In the beginning, for the sake of simplicity and control while waiting to see if the diet is working, parents usually choose simple meals that contain foods selected from the four basic exchange groups of the ketogenic diet:

- meat, fish, poultry, egg, or cheese (protein);
- fruits or vegetables (carbohydrate);
- butter, oil, margarine, or mayonnaise (fat);
- 36% to 40% heavy whipping cream (protein/carbohydrate/fat).

As long as all foods on the diet are calculated and weighed accurately on a gram scale to maintain the correct balance of fat, protein, and carbohydrates for the ketogenic ratio, the simple meal plans may be embellished with special treats such as shavings of baking chocolate or catsup. Note that flavorings such as baking chocolate, catsup, herbs and spices, lemon juice, and soy sauce contain carbohydrates. The overall carbohydrate level in the diet is extremely low, so a teaspoon of catsup calculated into a meal plan may cut your child's spinach allotment in half!

> It was very important to my son to feel as though he was getting a dessert. So I always keep a stock of homemade cream popsicles in the freezer, flavored with chocolate, which is calculated into his meal plans, and a little bit of saccharin. He gets one after every dinner. If he is supposed to have 80 cc. of cream and the Tupperware popsicle molds only hold 60 cc., then he drinks the rest of the cream straight.
>
> —CC

Parents learn as they go to judge what makes food sense and to balance their child's need for treats against the diet's restrictions. For older children whose calorie levels are higher, and for children in later phases of the diet when the ketogenic ratio is eased to 3:1 or 2:1, the amount and variety of foods allowed in the diet are greater.

One should think of the recipes included in this chapter in terms of entire meal plans, not single food items. The ketogenic ratio of food in the diet must balance within a whole meal, so any food calculated into one part of the meal affects what can go into other parts. For instance, baking chocolate shavings used to flavor the cream take away from carbohydrates that might otherwise have been eaten as fruit or vegetables. Pure vanilla flavoring, up to five drops a meal, has no countable food value and can be considered "free," which is to say not affecting the ketogenic balance of the meal. Each individual meal plan in the ketogenic diet has the same calorie level and the same ketogenic ratio. Each meal plan is interchangeable. There is no such thing as a small breakfast or a big dinner, saving food for later, or adding to a meal.

The menus that follow are examples drawn from the experience of various parents and are for a generic child. Your own meal plans will take into account your child's calorie level, protein needs, ketogenic ratio, and individual preferences. When a child has been seizure-free for a year and the physician allows the ketogenic ratio to be lowered to 3:1, larger portions of meat, fruit, and vegetables will be allowed to balance against less fat and cream, permitting greater variety and flexibility.

TIPS

The following are tips from parents who have experienced the diet:

- We started out with twenty to thirty menus, but came down to six or seven that he really loves, so that's all I prepare now.
- I use a salad plate so the amount of food seems larger.
- I fix six meals in advance and keep them in the refrigerator in carefully labeled Tupperware containers (breakfast, lunch, etc.) in case I am not there at mealtimes, or for when he goes to school or to a friend's house. I have built up a huge Tupperware collection.

- Use the spices that are allowed! A small amount goes a long way toward making the food interesting!
- My son will drink the cream straight down, but I often mix it with sugar-free soda so it will fill him up more.
- After cooking vegetables, remove as much water as possible to give your child more bulk. I drain cooked vegetables and pat out the water on a paper towel before weighing.
- I save two of his favorite meals and make them extra special. These two meals are used less than once a week so they remain special for times when we are having something he loves but cannot have, or for those times when nothing else sounds good to him.
- Chopped lettuce with mayonnaise can be a fairly large-looking element of a meal. It really helps fill up the plate, and it helps with bowel movements, too.
- Find places to hide the fat! Oil hides well in applesauce or ice cream. Butter disappears into peanut butter or cream cheese. Tuna, chicken, or egg salad eats up mayonnaise.
- Variety is very important. Mix two vegetables together. Select dishes that are familiar and resemble your family's normal meals. Try to be creative!
- Prepare entire meals in advance. Store them in microwaveable containers and reheat them in a microwave. This is especially helpful for school lunches, but it saves time anytime.
- You can make double-diluted, unsweetened Kool-Aid and sweeten it with saccharin if your child likes fruit-flavored drinks.
- If nasty-tasting medicine or supplements have to be mixed with food, don't spoil the little bit of fruit or vegetable your child gets. Mix the medicine with diluted cream instead.
- Do not buy diet foods—use real mayonnaise, butter, eggs, and so on. Diet foods tend to have high water content, and you want to give your child the benefits of as much pure fat, protein, carbohydrate, and calories as possible within the guidelines of the diet.
- Counter the small quantity of food with creative shapes and arrangement of food: slice meat thinly and fan it out. Pound chicken paper thin. Cut carrots into carrot chips, cucumbers into shoestring sticks.

BASIC TECHNIQUES

You will notice that the recipes in this chapter do not have quantities, as these must be calculated for each individual child. Each recipe is for a whole meal, considered as a unit, because foods in one part of the meal affect what can be included in another part while maintaining the prescribed ketogenic ratio. As a rule, ingredients such as catsup, lemon juice, vinegar, herbs and spices, soy sauce, and baking chocolate are used in two- to five-gram quantities (less than a teaspoon).

Meats should be lean with fat removed. Fish and poultry should be skinless and boneless. This is to ensure that the child's protein allotment will be as close to pure or solid protein as possible.

Cooked foods should be trimmed and weighed on the gram scale after cooking, except in the case of food that is heated only slightly or will not change volume during cooking (such as cheese for melting or eggs). Also, previously cooked foods that need only to be reheated in a microwave oven do not have to be weighed again after heating.

"What the eye sees, the mind remembers," the old adage goes. With a little practice, you will get used to judging how much twenty-five grams of chicken or fifteen grams of applesauce is. You will begin to get a feel for balancing a menu in terms of physical volume, color, texture, and flavor. However, never be tempted to "guesstimate" amounts for the sake of speed or efficiency. Always weigh for accuracy. The quantity of each ingredient in these menus varies from child to child, so we have not given exact amounts here. Quantities can be calculated either by hand or by using the computer program in consultation with a doctor or dietitian.

EXCHANGE LISTS

Traditionally, in the hand-calculated ketogenic diet, foods with similar protein, fat, and carbohydrate contents have been grouped into lists of items that may be substituted for one another interchangeably. When a menu calls for twenty-one grams of 10 percent fruit, you may choose cantaloupe, orange, strawberry, peach, or any other item from the 10 percent fruit list. Or you may choose to use fourteen grams (two-thirds

Figure 5. EXCHANGE LISTS

FRUIT OR JUICE: FRESH OR CANNED WITHOUT SUGAR

10% (Use amount prescribed)		15% (Use 2/3 amount prescribed)	
Applesauce, Mott's	Papaya	Apple	Kiwi
Cantaloupe	Peach	Apricot	Mango
Grapefruit	Strawberries	Blackberries	Nectarine
Grapes, purple	Tangerine	Blueberries	Pear
Honeydew melon	Watermelon	Figs	Pineapple
Orange		Grapes, green	Raspberries

VEGETABLES: FRESH, CANNED, OR FROZEN
Measure Raw (R) or Cooked (C) as Specified

Group A (Use twice amount prescribed)		Group B (Use amount prescribed)	
Asparagus /C	Radish /R	Beets /C	Kohlrabi /C
Beet greens /C	Rhubarb /R	Broccoli /C	Mushroom /R
Cabbage /C	Sauerkraut /C	Brussels sprouts /C	Mustard greens /C
Celery /C or R	Summer squash /C	Cabbage /R	Okra /C
Chicory /R	Swiss chard /C	Carrots /R or C	Onion /R or C
Cucumbers /R	Tomato /R	Cauliflower /C	Rutabaga /C
Eggplant /C	Tomato juice	Collards /C	Spinach /C
Endive /R	Turnips /C	Dandelion greens /C	Tomato /C
Green pepper /R or C	Turnip greens /C	Green beans /C	Winter squash/C
Poke /C	Watercress /R	Kale /C	

FAT
Unsaturated fats are recommended

CHEESE

Bacon fat	Canola oil	American
Butter	Corn oil	Cheddar
Margarine	Olive oil	Monterey Jack
Mayonnaise	Peanut oil	

MEAT, FISH, AND POULTRY

Beef	Pork (fresh or cured)
Chicken	Tuna (canned, packed in water not in oil)
Fish	Turkey
Lamb	Veal

the amount prescribed) of a 15 percent fruit, such as blueberries, pear, or pineapple. Similarly, if a menu calls for eighteen grams of a Group B vegetable, you may choose any item or combination of items from the Group B list, including broccoli, carrots, or green beans. Or you may choose to use twice that amount, thirty-six grams, of any Group A vegetable or combination of Group A vegetables, including asparagus, celery, and summer squash. When the meal plan calls for fat, you may use any fat or combination of fats such as margarine, mayonnaise, or oil. We suggest that you use monounsaturated fats, such as canola and olive oil, as often as possible.

The meat, fish, and poultry list includes a variety of lean meats similar to one another in protein content. Bacon, which has a much higher fat content, must be calculated separately from other meats, as must processed meats such as bologna, hot dogs, and sausage, which vary widely according to the manufacturer's contents. Other foods commonly used on the diet that do not fit into any of the exchange lists include peanut butter, eggs, cottage cheese, Parmesan cheese, sour cream, and cream cheese.

The function of exchange lists is to make hand-calculated meal planning easier. The diet works well with this method, in spite of minor variations in the makeup of each Group A vegetable and 10 percent fruit.

Using the computer program for calculations gives greater precision in adjusting the precise number of grams of protein and carbohydrate in each vegetable or fruit. No evidence exists to show that this accuracy alone affects the performance of the diet, but there is value in consistency. Once the diet is calculated, whether by hand or by computer, you may use the exchange lists.

MIX AND MATCH

One way to think about planning menus is to translate generic meals into food that the child likes to eat. Meal plans are usually written in terms of their basic nutritive composition—protein, fat, carbohydrate. With a little imagination, these plans become meals that resemble those eaten by the rest of the family:

PLANS	MEALS

PLANS

1. Meat/fish/poultry, fruit, fat, cream
2. Egg, fruit, fat, cream
3. Cheese, fruit, fat, cream
4. Meat/fish/poultry, vegetable, fat, cream
5. Egg, vegetable, fat, cream
6. Cheese, vegetable, fat, cream

MEALS

1. Steak with peaches and whipped cream
2. Scrambled egg with butter, orange juice, cream
3. Fruit-topped cheesecake
4. Broiled flounder with broccoli and parfait
5. Mushroom omelette with shake
6. Eggplant pizza with vanilla shake

Another way to think up menus is to mix and match one item from each of four basic columns. Column A is protein, Column B is carbohydrate, Column C is cream, and Column D is fat. Choose one item from Column A, one or two items from Column B, and one item each from Columns C and D. Use them in any combination to produce a variety of menus.

PROTEIN COLUMN A	CARBOHYDRATE COLUMN B	CREAM COLUMN C	FAT COLUMN D
Broiled chicken	Asparagus	Ice cream	Mayonnaise
Sliced steak	Summer squash	Popsicle	Butter
Fish filet	Mashed turnip	Vanilla shake	Oil
Pork chop	Cucumber/tomato	Maple walnut whip	
Ground beef	Green pepper	Cream in diet soda	

• •

DON'T FORGET

A sugarless multivitamin with iron and a calcium supplement must be taken every day to be nutritionally complete!

• •

SCRAMBLED EGG BREAKFAST

INGREDIENTS:

Egg	Cream
Butter	Orange juice

OPTIONS:

Crisp bacon, ham, or sausage

Grated cheese in omelettes

Vegetables, fresh fruit, or applesauce instead of juice

Baking chocolate for cocoa

Beat equal amounts of yolk and white. Cook eggs in a microwave or nonstick pan, which may be sprayed with nonstick vegetable oil. Transfer to scale and weigh, trimming if necessary. Egg may also be weighed uncooked and then fried with some of allowed fat. Transfer to plate and add any additional butter. For omelettes, egg should be cooked flat and thin, then put back in pan, filled with calculated cheese or vegetable/butter mixture, heated slightly, and scraped thoroughly onto a plate with a small rubber spatula. Garnish plate with calculated crisp bacon and/or grated cheese sprinkles. Dilute cream with water or ice to make it more like milk, or make hot chocolate by melting baking chocolate shavings in cream with sweetener. Your child must consume all the butter on the plate. Drink orange juice or eat fruit last for dessert. Eggs may be weighed either before or after cooking. If they are weighed before cooking, you may include some of the allowed fat in the cooking. If you choose to include bacon or cheese, less egg will be allowed in the meal plan because the protein allotment will be shared.

WESTERN OMELETTE

INGREDIENTS:

Egg	Tomato
Mayonnaise	Green pepper
Cream	Onion
Dill, basil, salt, pepper	

Scramble egg and weigh. Add a little of allotted cream and scramble again. Pour into heated pan coated with vegetable cooking spray. Chop

FRIED EGG TECHNIQUE: If a whole egg is more than a child is allowed, separate egg first. Weigh an equal amount of white and yolk. Add a little cream to the yolk. Heat oil in a skillet. Place round cookie cutter in center. Pour white around outside of the cookie cutter and pour yolk mixture inside. Remove cookie cutter. Fry as normal.

vegetables. Sprinkle with pinch of spices. Mix with mayonnaise. Spread vegetable/mayonnaise mixture on egg. Then flip top over to make omelette and cook a few more minutes until done. This omelette may also be made in a sandwich machine by pouring half of the egg on the grid, spreading the vegetable mixture on top, then adding the other half of the egg and closing the machine until done.

EASY APPLE-SAUSAGE BAKE

INGREDIENTS:

Unsweetened applesauce

Bob Evans sausage link

Butter

Cream

Sweetener, vanilla

Speck of cinnamon

Broil sausage link under medium flame until brown, boil until done, or sauté in frying pan. Drain on paper towel. Weigh and trim. Meanwhile, place applesauce in small ovenproof container. Mix in brown sugar substitute or sweetener, top with butter, and place under broiler. Whip cream until it thickens, add a few drops of vanilla and sweetener, and continue beating until stiff. When applesauce is warm and butter is melted, top with whipped cream and dust with cinnamon. Serve with sausage.

STRAWBERRY CHOCOLATE CHIP ICE CREAM WITH BACON

(Christopher's favorite breakfast)

INGREDIENTS:

Bacon

Strawberries

Cream

Canola oil

Vanilla, sweetener

Baking chocolate

Ice cream can be made up to a week beforehand: Dissolve saccharin tablet in $\frac{1}{2}$ teaspoon of warm water. Add to cream in a small Pyrex dish. Flavor with vanilla to taste, baking chocolate shavings, and sliced fresh strawberries. Freeze about 1 hour, or until ice begins to form. Remove from freezer. Stir in canola oil quickly and return to freezer. Unmold and serve in a small bowl with crisp bacon on the side.

Vary the fruit (peach, raspberry), omit the chocolate or melt it into cream, or add pure maple extract and chopped nuts for variety. Omitting chocolate or substituting chopped nuts for fruit has to be calculated, of course. Cream may be whipped before freezing.

QUICHE LORRAINE (CUSTARD WITH BACON)

INGREDIENTS:

Egg

Cream

Bacon

Orange

Heat cream to scald. Do not boil. Stir beaten egg into cream. Stir in crumbled bacon. Pour mixture into a custard cup. Place in a pan of water. Microwave or bake at 350° until done (about 25 minutes, or until a silver knife inserted in the middle comes out clean). Serve in the custard cup in the middle of a small plate, with thin orange slices arranged around the cup in the shape of a flower.

TUNA SALAD PLATE

INGREDIENTS:

Tuna	Mayonnaise
Cream	Sugarless Jell-O
Sour cream	Parmesan cheese
Baking chocolate	Cheez Whiz
Cucumber, tomato, celery, lettuce	

Mix mayonnaise and tuna; arrange in center of plate. Stir together sour cream, Cheez Whiz, and Parmesan; mix with chopped lettuce and arrange around tuna. Garnish plate with cucumbers and tomatoes. For dessert, sugarless Jell-O topped with sweetened vanilla whipped cream, sprinkled with baking chocolate shavings. Hard-boiled egg, cubed chicken or turkey, or baby shrimps may be substituted for the tuna. These salads are easy to prepare in advance, making them ideal travel or school meals.

PEANUT BUTTER CELERY BOATS

INGREDIENTS:

Celery strips

Peanut butter

Cream

1 chopped walnut

Sweetener

Speck of cinnamon

Unsweetened applesauce butter

Wash thin celery ribs. Peel to remove any strings. Slice off

Applesauce is a great place to hide fat. As much as equal parts fat to applesauce will blend in and taste good. Add ¼ grain of saccharin dissolved in warm water or a dash of liquid sweetener to unsweetened applesauce and dust with a speck of cinnamon before serving. May be served warm or at room temperature.

bottom for better stability. Weigh and trim. Combine peanut butter with half of allotted butter. Mix thoroughly. Fill the cavity of celery ribs with peanut butter-butter mixture. Cut into 3-inch pieces. Arrange on "waves" of lettuce strips. Meanwhile, heat unsweetened applesauce gently with other half of butter. Top warm applesauce with sweetened whipped cream. Dust with cinnamon and chopped walnut. Celery may also be stuffed with tuna and mayonnaise to make tuna boats.

CHEF'S SALAD WITH MAPLE WALNUT WHIP

INGREDIENTS:

American cheese

Ham and/or turkey

Lettuce, olive

Oil

Vinegar

Cucumber, celery, green pepper

Tomato, mushroom, carrot

Cream

Crushed walnut

Pure maple extract, sweetener

Combine chopped lettuce and sliced celery, green pepper, mushrooms, and carrots in a bowl. Arrange tomato and cucumber slices, olive, and strips of cheese, ham, and/or turkey on top. Shake or beat with a fork the oil and vinegar, a speck of salt and pepper, and a few flakes of oregano in a jar with a tight lid (mayonnaise may be substituted for some of the oil for thicker consistency). Pour over salad. Sprinkle a few parsley flakes and a dash of Accent over all. For dessert: whip cream until thick. Add 3 or 4 drops of pure maple extract and a few drops of sweetener, and continue whipping until stiff. (Several grams vegetable oil may also be whipped into cream if there is too much oil for the salad.) Heap into a parfait dish. Sprinkle with crushed walnuts and serve. Or use butterscotch extract and chopped pecans instead for Butterscotch Fluff.

Weigh all Group A vegetables together and weigh all Group B vegetables together. You can also weigh cheese, turkey, and/or ham strips together as these are exchangeable proteins. The olive or walnut can be thrown in as a free food.

SPINACH SALAD

INGREDIENTS:

Hard-boiled egg

Spinach

Crisp bacon

Mushroom, carrot, red onion

Olive oil, vinegar

Dried mustard, garlic salt

Cream

Saltine or oyster cracker

Butter

Vanilla, sweetener

Wash spinach, chop coarsely, place in bowl. Sprinkle with chopped red onion, sliced mushroom, and carrot. Shake oil and vinegar together in a jar with a speck of dried mustard, garlic salt, and pepper. Pour over salad. Sprinkle with crumbled crisp bacon and chopped egg (equal parts white and yolk). Spread allowed saltine or oyster cracker with butter. Serve with vanilla shake or popsicle.

DEVILED EGG WITH BERRY PARFAIT

INGREDIENTS:

Hard boiled egg

Carrots, celery, onion

Butter, mayonnaise

Dried mustard, paprika

Grated lemon rind

Lettuce, parsley

Cream

Vanilla, sweetener, chocolate

Cut egg in half lengthwise, and weigh equal amounts of white and yolk. Mix yolk thoroughly with mayonnaise, a few grams melted butter, a speck of dried mustard, chopped celery, and onion. Spoon yolk mixture back into the egg white. Sprinkle with salt and pepper. Dust with paprika. Serve on a plate with chopped lettuce mixed with mayonnaise and vinegar, and a few sprigs of calculated parsley. For dessert, add vanilla and sweetener to cream and whip until stiff. Alternate whipped cream in a parfait dish with layers of sliced raspberries or strawberries.

Smaller children or those on a higher ketogenic ratio may not be allotted enough carbohydrates for a saltine cracker. In this case, use more oil and/or mayonnaise in the dressing instead of the butter, or whip a little canola oil into the shake.

At one point my son started gaining weight and I couldn't figure out why. Then Mrs. Kelly and I reviewed everything I was doing. I had started hiding a lot of fat in ice cream in the form of canola oil because my son had gotten tired of eating so much butter on top of everything. But I was measuring the oil, like the cream and juice, by volume. Lighter liquids are approximately equal when measured either by weight or by volume. But because it is so heavy, oil has to be measured by weight on a gram scale. When I started measuring the canola oil on the gram scale instead of in the graduated cylinder, the weight gain stopped.

—JS

CUCUMBER BOATS WITH WALNUT MERINGUES

INGREDIENTS:

Cucumber	Egg white
Cream cheese	Walnuts, chopped
Mayonnaise	Butter
Cream	Strawberries

Peel a small cucumber. Slice lengthwise. With a teaspoon, hollow out seeds and discard. Weigh and trim. In a small bowl, mix together cream cheese, mayonnaise, butter, and sour cream. Pack into hollowed cucumber. Arrange on banana split plate with a lettuce leaf spread with any extra mayonnaise. For fun, pierce a triangle of colored paper with a toothpick and fly a flag from the front of the "boat." Meanwhile, beat egg whites until stiff. Add chopped walnuts, $\frac{1}{4}$ grain saccharin dissolved in 1 teaspoon

In the absence of toast, it's nice to have something crispy that holds a shape, like celery or cucumber boats.

—JS

warm water or less, and a drop or 2 of vanilla if desired. Drop by the teaspoon on a nonstick pan sprayed with Pam. Broil for 3 to 4 minutes or until golden brown. Whip strawberries and cream together for a strawberry shake. Bigger children, with their larger protein allotment, can have more of a meal along with their walnut meringues, but for smaller children the egg whites will take up most of the protein allotment.

COTTAGE CHEESE WITH VEGETABLES

INGREDIENTS:

Cottage cheese	Carrots
Mayonnaise	Cucumber
Butter	Radish
Cream	Chopped walnut
Maple flavoring	

Chop vegetables into small cubes. Mix butter and mayonnaise together. Stir butter and mayonnaise into cottage cheese. Stir in vegetables. Season with a speck of salt and pepper. Whip cream with allowed sweetener and maple flavoring and sprinkle with chopped walnut.

CHICKEN SOUP AND CUSTARD

INGREDIENTS:

Custard
Soup
Egg
Diced chicken
Cream
Granulated bouillon
Salt (a speck)
Carrots, celery, lettuce
Saccharin (1/8 grain)
Butter, mayonnaise

Custard: Scald 3 parts cream to 1 part water. Combine with 2 parts beaten egg, salt, saccharin, and vanilla. Pour into a cup and bake in a shallow pan of water 25 minutes at 350° or until done (knife inserted in center will come out clean).

Soup: Dissolve broth in 1/2 cup hot water. Add enough chicken to make up the protein left over from the egg (if any), and carrots and celery to fill the carbohydrate allotment. Melt a little butter into the soup, and spread the rest of the fat as mayonnaise on lettuce. Drink any leftover cream as beverage.

In summer, a glass of decaffeinated tea with ice and a twist of lemon rind makes a thirst-quenching drink.

In the chicken soup recipe, the carrots can also be made into sticks and eaten dipped in mayonnaise instead of being diced into the soup.

CREAM OF TOMATO SOUP WITH ICE CREAM

INGREDIENTS:

Tomato sauce

Cream

Mayonnaise, oil

Cheese (strips or grated)

Celery, onion

Speck of tarragon, salt, pepper

Lettuce leaf

Baking chocolate, sweetener

Sauté celery and onion in about 5 grams butter. Add tomato sauce. Add a speck each of tarragon, salt, and pepper. Add half of cream allotment and water to thin to desired consistency. Stir until smooth and heat until warm. Serve with chopped lettuce mixed with mayonnaise on the side topped with cheese strips, or sprinkle hot soup with grated cheese. For dessert, melt baking chocolate shavings into rest of cream and pour into bowl of ice cream scoop. Chill for 1 hour. Stir in canola oil quickly and return to freezer. Freeze until hard.

BAKED EGG WITH CHEESE

INGREDIENTS:

Beaten egg	Cream
Cheddar cheese	Butter
Asparagus, carrots	Lettuce
Vanilla, sweetener	Lemon rind

Butter a small ovenproof dish with about 5 grams butter. Beat together egg, about 15 grams cream, and grated cheese. Bake 12 to 15 minutes at 325° or until cheese is melted. Let cool slightly. Serve in baking dish on larger plate garnished with steamed vegetables such as asparagus and carrots topped with lemon rind butter (butter melted with a small amount of grated lemon rind). In a blender, blend rest of cream with a few drops of vanilla and sweetener and 2 ice cubes until ice is ground into a frothy vanilla shake.

For a variety of cream soups, asparagus, broccoli, or spinach may be substituted for the tomato.

EASTERN SHORE BLUE PLATE

INGREDIENTS:

Oscar Mayer beef bologna

Cheez Whiz

Olive

Mushroom, green pepper

Butter

Celery, tomato

Cream

D-Zerta gelatin

Place two leaves of iceberg lettuce in a small plate or bowl. Top with the bologna, sliced vegetables, and Cheez Whiz. Sprinkle with a speck of Season-All. Microwave for about 1 minute or until cheese melts. Serve with sugarless gelatin topped with whipped cream.

PARMESAN "SPAGHETTI"

INGREDIENTS:

Spaghetti squash	Cream
Parmesan cheese	Butter
Lettuce	Mayonnaise

Boil squash (raw squash may be frozen in individual portions in advance). Drain well and weigh. Melt butter on top; sprinkle grated cheese plus a little pepper and oregano if desired. Stir to make a paste (paste may also be made in a separate pan with a tablespoon of the cream beaten into the Parmesan-butter). Mix chopped lettuce with dressing made of one or more of the following: mayonnaise, sour cream, Cheez Whiz, vinegar, cottage cheese. Pour cream in pineapple-orange soda and whip lightly in blender for a frothy dessert.

"SPAGHETTI" WITH TOMATO SAUCE

INGREDIENTS:

Bean sprouts

Olive oil

Canned tomatoe

Dash of spices, garlic

Cream

Ground beef

Lettuce

Parmesan cheese

If taken to school in an insulated bag, the Blue Plate can be eaten warm at lunch. A most versatile dish—bacon or any meat may be substituted for bologna, and any combination of vegetables may be used. Other brands of bologna may be used if you calculate the meal plan based on accurate information about each brand's content.

Whole cooked tomatoes may be mashed to create a sauce instead of using commercial tomato products.

Heat olive oil in a saucepan. Add a clove of garlic and sauté until brown. Remove garlic. Mash the tomatoes to a pulp, add to oil, and stir over low heat. Add a dash of basil and oregano. Meanwhile, roll ground beef into a ball, sprinkle with salt and pepper, and boil in water 5 to 10 minutes. Drain and pat dry on paper towels, then weigh for allotted protein and trim. Add to sauce and heat. Meanwhile, cover bean sprouts with cold water and bring to a boil, then simmer about 10 minutes. Drain thoroughly. Weigh. Place on a plate and cover with sauce. Top with a dash of grated Parmesan cheese if desired. For dessert, a pre-made chocolate popsicle: heat cream with grated baking chocolate until chocolate melts. Stir in a few drops vanilla and sweetener. Pour into popsicle mold and freeze. This may be made up to a week in advance.

"LINGUINE" WITH TOMATO SAUCE

INGREDIENTS:

Celery

Tomato sauce

Olive oil

Cream

Ground beef

Parmesan cheese

Oregano, pepper

Granulated beef bouillon

Peel celery to remove strings. Slice lengthwise into very thin strips. Weigh. Boil about an inch of water in a pot with a small amount of granulated beef bouillon. Add the celery "linguine" and cook until soft. In a small skillet, heat together the tomato sauce, olive oil, cooked beef, speck of oregano, and pepper. Pour over linguine and top with grated cheese. Serve vanilla cream popsicle or frozen cream shake for dessert.

Even the smallest sprinkle of Parmesan cheese has to be calculated into the diet. Meat balls can be frozen for later use.

I bought the kind of blender that's a wand you can stick right into a tall glass. You just rinse the wand off in the sink after you use it. That way I don't have to wash the whole blender every time.

—FD

HOT DOG AND CATSUP

INGREDIENTS:

Hebrew National hot dog

Butter

Cream cheese

Zucchini or asparagus

Heavy cream

Lettuce

Catsup

Baking chocolate

Ritz Bits

Vanilla, sweetener

Boil hot dog, drain, weigh, and trim. Cut into thin slices; dab catsup on each slice. Arrange on a small plate. Spread cream cheese (with some of the butter mixed in if desired) on lettuce. Steam vegetables; top with rest of butter. Serve with allowed Ritz Bits. For dessert, melt baking chocolate in cream, add a few drops vanilla and a little sweetener, and pour into a popsicle mold. Freeze until hard (this popsicle may be made up to a week in advance). Mix any remaining cream in up to 120 grams of diet soda for a refreshing drink.

SAUSAGE WITH SAUERKRAUT

INGREDIENTS:

Sausage or hot dog

Mustard or catsup

Cream

Sauerkraut

Butter

Oil

With commercial products such as hot dogs, the brand must always be specified. Brands of hot dog other than Hebrew National may be used in this recipe if calculations are based on accurate information about the specified brand.

Slice sausage or hot dog into $\frac{1}{4}$-inch slices and combine with sauerkraut in a small saucepan. Add 1 inch of water and bring to a boil. Reduce heat and simmer for 25 minutes. Drain and weigh the sausage and sauerkraut separately. Add butter and stir until melted. Serve with allotted mustard or catsup on the side whipped with a few grams oil, if desired. Freeze cream in ice cream scoop and float in mug of diet root beer.

PEPPER STEAK STIR FRY AND BAVARIAN CREAM

INGREDIENTS:

Thin sliced beef

Green pepper

Onions

Mushrooms

Vanilla

Sweetener

Lettuce

Gelatin

Baking chocolate

Butter, oil

Dash of soy sauce

Bavarian cream: Swell 2 grams of gelatin with 2 tablespoons cold water. Add 2 grams baking chocolate and a little of allotted butter. Place over warm water until baking chocolate, butter, and gelatin are melted. Stir in 1/4 grain saccharin, a few drops vanilla, and cream. Pour into mold and freeze until hardened.

Stir fry: Heat oil equal to remaining fat allotment after butter used in Bavarian (some fat may be reserved for use as oil or mayonnaise in salad dressing). Sauté onions, mushrooms, and green pepper. Season with a speck of salt, pepper, and a dash of soy sauce. Cook beef separately in broiler or microwave. Weigh. Add to vegetables and serve. On the side, serve a chopped lettuce leaf with any remaining oil or mayonnaise for dressing.

In the Bavarian cream meal, total fat allotment is divided into three dishes. You can decide how much butter to melt into the Bavarian, how much oil to use with the stir fry, and how much oil or mayonnaise to use as salad dressing as long as all fats add up to the correct total.

BURGER WITH "POTATO SALAD"

INGREDIENTS:

Ground beef	Zucchini
Catsup	Mayonnaise, oil
Salt, pepper	Oregano
Cream	Lettuce
Vanilla, sweetener	Sugar-free Jell-O

Flatten the ground beef into a ¼-inch thick burger. Heat a nonstick skillet with a few drops of the allotted oil or cooking spray. Sauté the burger 1 to 1½ minutes on each side. Weigh the sautéed burger and trim. Meanwhile, measure the catsup and beat in an equal amount of oil. Steam zucchini. Weigh and cut into 1/2-inch cubes. Mix the zucchini with mayonnaise, oregano, and a pinch of salt and pepper. Arrange the beef on a lettuce leaf. Spread catsup mixture on steak.

For dessert, top sugar-free Jell-O with whipped sweetened vanilla cream.

"FREE" WAYS TO DRESS UP YOUR CREAM

Ice cream ball
- Dust with a speck of cinnamon or nutmeg
- Flavor with sweetener and vanilla or calculated baking chocolate
- Whip in canola oil after one hour of freezing

Popsicle
- Dilute cream with water for bigger popsicle
- Flavor with sweetener and vanilla or calculated baking chocolate

Whipped parfait
- Layer with calculated berries
- Sprinkle with a chopped nut
- Flavor with sweetener and vanilla, lemon, maple, almond, or coconut extract
- Serve on top of calculated sugar-free Jell-O

Cream soda
- Pour cream into fruit-flavored sugar-free soda

"PIZZA"

INGREDIENTS:
Thin eggplant slice
Olive oil
Tomato puree
Mozzarella cheese
Cream
Lettuce
Speck of oregano
Vanilla, sweetener

Brush eggplant slice with a little olive oil and broil on both sides until golden. Mix remaining olive oil with tomato sauce; spread on eggplant in a thin layer. Sprinkle with a speck of oregano. Cover with grated cheese. Broil until melted. Serve with diluted cream shake.

BROILED FISH WITH TARTAR SAUCE

INGREDIENTS:
Flounder or other fish
Asparagus
Lettuce
Sugarless Jell-O
Tartar sauce
Mayonnaise, butter
Cream
Accent, pepper

Broil the fish about 8 minutes or until flaky. Season with a speck of Accent and pepper. Spread with measured tartar sauce. Meanwhile, steam asparagus about 5 minutes or until done. For mock hollandaise sauce, divide remaining fat allotment equally into butter and mayonnaise. Melt butter with a piece of lemon rind. Remove rind. Beat in mayonnaise with fork. Beat in a few drops warm water if consistency is too thick. Arrange flounder on a small plate with asparagus topped with sauce. Serve sugarless Jell-O topped with whipped cream for dessert. As an alternative to steamed asparagus, try sautéed mushrooms and onions in butter. If butter in vegetables is too much, hide some fat as canola oil whipped into the cream before freezing.

A tomato slice may be substituted for the eggplant. Triangular slices of cheese can also make a fun pretend pizza!

Robert doesn't like cream. Any way you fix it, it's one of his "gag" foods. I tried every way imaginable to fix it. I tried blending it into shakes, adding ice cubes, vanilla flavoring, saccharin, pureed fruit. Gag! I tried using cream to make cheese sauce for vegetables, making cream soups, adding it to beef stew, freezing it into ice cream, whipping it with gelatin and cream cheese to make "pink fluff." Gag! Robert never liked fatty foods much. I finally realized: why knock yourself out if he's never going to like it—just fix the easiest thing he'll accept. So now I just add Diet Faygo to the cream and shake. Sometimes I add a little oil, too, to complete a meal plan. Robert still is not wild about the cream, but he accepts it. His favorite flavor of Faygo is orange, but sometimes I use root beer or chocolate cream soda for variety. Now I don't have to worry about carting around blenders or "pink fluff" not surviving the cooler.

—CC

CHICKEN FINGERS AND COLE SLAW

INGREDIENTS:

Chicken breast

Scallion

Dry mustard, tarragon

Cream

Cabbage, carrot

Mayonnaise

Butter

Vanilla, sweetener

Heat a few drops oil in a nonstick skillet. Sauté chicken breast at medium-high heat for about 3 minutes per side or until lightly

I don't cook with butter as the allowed fat. Since the fat is his body fuel, I want him to get as much as possible. When you cook with butter, you can easily lose some of it in the pan. I usually just spray the pan with nonstick aerosol spray, cook the food, and add the butter while it's hot.

—EH

browned. Remove chicken from heat; weigh and trim. Turn heat off. Add butter (⅓ of fat allotment) to skillet. Add a dash of mustard, tarragon, and garlic salt. Stir until butter is melted. Remove skillet from heat. Cut chicken breast into thin strips or very thin slices and fan out on a small plate. Pour butter sauce over chicken. Meanwhile, chop cabbage (red or green) with a little grated carrot, thinly sliced scallion, and a leaf of lettuce. Mix mayonnaise (⅔ of fat allotment) with a couple of grams of vinegar. Stir in cabbage mixture. Sprinkle with salt, pepper, and a few parsley flakes. Serve with frozen vanilla-flavored cream ball.

BEEF STEW

INGREDIENTS:

Roast beef	Pearl onions
Cabbage	Cherry tomatoes
Turnips	Cream
Baking chocolate	Sweetener

Steam cabbage, turnip, and onion until tender. Place them in a small, nonstick pot (such as a one-cup Pyrex) with the roast beef and ¼ cup water. Add butter and sprinkle with a speck of salt and pepper. Simmer 15 minutes. For thicker sauce, mash some turnip into the liquid. Place cherry tomato halves around a small plate and spoon stew in center. Serve with chocolate ice cream.

CHICKEN CUTLET WITH APPLE À LA MODE

INGREDIENTS:

Chicken
Sour cream and Cheez Whiz
Butter
Lettuce
Cream
Cinnamon
Saccharin
Apple slice

Chicken cutlet: Pound the chicken very thin between sheets of waxed paper. Grill or pan fry for 1 minute on each side. Sprinkle with a speck of seasoned salt or salt and pepper, and dot with some of allotted butter if desired. Spread lettuce leaf with Cheez Whiz, roll into a pinwheel, cut in half, and arrange on small plate with chicken.

Apple à la mode: Cut center slice from a small apple. Leave skin on, remove core, and weigh. Sauté in remaining butter in a small skillet until soft. Dust with a speck of cinnamon. Place apple slice in an ice cream dish and top with a ball of sweetened vanilla frozen cream. Pour any cinnamon butter remaining in skillet on top of ice cream. (*Optional:* Serve with Shasta Red Apple diet drink.)

Any meat, fish, or poultry may be substituted for the chicken in this recipe.

Chris loved mashed buttered turnips because they reminded him of potatoes, and he loved potatoes even though he couldn't have them.

—JS

CHICKEN WITH MASHED TURNIPS

INGREDIENTS:

Chicken breast
Turnips
Butter
Coconut extract
Cream

Broil chicken breast or sauté it in a nonstick skillet with a few drops of oil. Season chicken with a few flakes of tarragon or oregano if desired. Boil turnips until soft. Mash with butter. Season with salt and pepper. Serve with a chopped lettuce leaf and coconut milk: dilute cream with water to taste. Add a few drops Sucaryl, 2-3 drops pure coconut extract, and a speck of nutmeg.

Every weekend I would make twenty-one ice cream servings. My son didn't like much fat in his meals, so I hid almost all of it in the ice cream, which he loved and ate with every meal. I had to plan my menus in advance so I would know how much fat I had to hide in the ice cream for each meal. Mostly I used canola oil, which whips into the cream beautifully just before it freezes. There would be different quantities of oil whipped in with the cream, depending on each menu. Sometimes I would choose a menu with fruit and make strawberry ice cream. I had to label the ice cream very carefully as to which day and which meal they were made for.

—JS

LAMB WITH CUCUMBER AND TOMATO

INGREDIENTS:

Lamb chop	Cucumber
Mayonnaise	Tomato
Vinegar	Baking chocolate
Olive oil	Cream

Broil lamb chop 5 minutes on each side. Season with a speck of pepper and Accent or rosemary if desired. Trim and weigh lamb. Slice meat thinly and fan out on plate. Cut cucumber and tomato into $\frac{1}{2}$-inch cubes. Combine vinegar and olive oil and pour over cucumber-tomato salad. Serve with a chopped or rolled lettuce leaf spread with mayonnaise and a chocolate popsicle.

"TACOS"

INGREDIENTS:

Ground beef

Chopped tomato

Lettuce

Grated cheese or sour cream

Cream

Speck of chili powder

Cook beef in nonstick pan. Weigh. Dust beef with a speck of chili powder. Roll beef, tomato, and cheese or sour cream in lettuce leaf. Pour cream into up to 120 grams of orange diet soda for a dessert drink.

CHEESECAKE: A BIRTHDAY MEAL!

Adjust for each child's individual meal plan requirements. For 1,000 calorie recipe, use:

INGREDIENTS:

Egg   5

Butter   11

Cottage cheese   13

Cream   50

Sour cream   6

Fruit   14

Cream cheese   14

Vanilla, sweetener   5 drops

Mix together all ingredients except fruit. Add vanilla to taste and $\frac{1}{2}$ grain of saccharin dissolved in $\frac{1}{2}$ teaspoon of warm water or liquid sweetener to taste. Bake in small, greased Pyrex dish at 350° for 25 minutes or until light golden on top. Cool. Arrange fruit slices on top—sliced strawberries, pineapple, or peach. Makes a whole meal! Save a bit of cream to whip and pile on top for extra excitement.

Adjust for each child's individual meal plan requirements.

Because cream contains so much fat, the more cream you use the less oil, mayonnaise, and butter you will have to fit into the rest of the menu. But if your child doesn't mind eating a lot of mayonnaise or butter, you can use less cream and fill out the carbohydrate allotment with more vegetables or fruit.

THANKSGIVING CUSTARD

INGREDIENTS:

Canned pumpkin

Cream

Beaten egg

Melted butter, mayonnaise

Chicken bouillon

Speck of ginger, nutmeg, cinnamon

Sweetener

Warm cream. Stir in rest of ingredients. Use approximately 3 parts cream to 2 parts pumpkin and 1 part beaten egg. Pour into ovenproof ramekin. Bake in 325° oven for 30 minutes or until set. Serve with a warm cup of turkey broth and a lettuce leaf with mayonnaise.

KETOGENIC EGGNOG—36% CREAM

Keto 5:1	Keto 4:1	Keto 3:1
90 g. cream	60 g. cream	80 g. cream
19 g. egg	25 g. egg	65 g. egg
vanilla	vanilla	vanilla
saccharin	saccharin	saccharin
Calories 340	Calories 245	Calories 365
Pro 4.1	Pro 4.2	Pro 9.4
Fat 34.7	Fat 24.6	Fat 36.6
Carb 2.7	Carb 1.8	Carb 2.4

Beat egg slightly. Weigh. Dissolve artificial sweetener in 1 teaspoon or more water. Add to cream. Combine egg, cream, vanilla, and sweetener to taste. Whip lightly if desired. Sprinkle with nutmeg. Use as travel meal or for an occasional snack.

A cheesecake meal is easy to carry to school in its container for special occasions, such as when other kids are eating cake to celebrate a birthday.

QUESTIONS ABOUT PREPARING THE DIET

1. Is it good to use high-fat meats to increase the fat content of the diet?

Protein is very important for your child's growth. The protein portion of the diet should therefore be close to pure. Meat should be lean, trimmed of fat. Chicken and fish should be without skin. Cooked fat may be trimmed off and measured separately as part of the fat allotment for the meal. High-fat processed meats such as sausage and bologna should be calculated in the menu according to the manufacturer's contents.

2. What if some of the food sticks to the pan?

Use nonstick pans and nonstick spray, and scrape out as much as possible with a small rubber spatula. Cook at low temperatures to avoid burning. Better yet, prepare food using nonstick methods: bake or broil meats, microwave eggs, steam vegetables. Remember that the allotted weights are for cooked food unless otherwise indicated, so until you are experienced with the difference between raw and cooked weights, your meats and vegetables or fruits should be prepared and cooked separately and then assembled with fats at the end.

Like the cheesecake, frozen eggnog in a margarine tub makes a great birthday party food. Try decorating top with fruit (strawberries, cherries). Wrap the margarine tub in colored foil and take it to school for birthday parties.

3. Should I try to use margarine instead of butter?

We recommend that you use as many unsaturated fats as possible, such as canola or olive oil, or margarine made from canola oil. However, no data indicate that the ketogenic diet, despite its high fat content, leads to heart disease or atherosclerosis later in life.

4. My child is too disabled to care much what she eats, so I just want the simplest menu to prepare. What is easiest?

The simplest ketogenic menu planning involves using the four main food lists of the diet without embellishment:

Protein (meat, fish, chicken, cheese, egg)
Carbohydrate (fruit or vegetable)
Fat (butter, margarine, mayonnaise, oil)
Cream

It takes very little time to broil a bit of meat or chicken, steam a piece of broccoli or cut up a tomato, put butter on the chicken or mayonnaise on the broccoli, and serve with a cup of cream diluted with ice and water. For a softer consistency, try fruit-topped cheesecake or custard with bacon and cooked vegetables.

5. What if the family has to travel or I don't have time to prepare a meal?

The eggnog recipe (see p.60) is a very good emergency or convenience food on the ketogenic diet. It can be made in advance and taken along in a Thermos or container. You should not use eggnog too often in the diet, but it may always be used in a pinch. Make up to two days' meals ahead of time when traveling and take them along in a portable cooler. Ask restaurants to microwave them for you if appropriate. Tuna salad with sliced vegetables such as celery, cucumbers, or carrots is especially mobile. See Chapter 7 for further details.

6. Can I decrease the amount of cream and use more fat in a given menu?

Cream is made up of protein, carbohydrate, and fat. You cannot simply use more fat and less cream because then the carbohydrate and protein content of the meal would be inaccurate. Ask your dietitian to calculate a meal plan that uses less cream but still distributes carbohydrate, protein, and fat in the proper ketogenic ratio.

Process

Section II

Initiating the Ketogenic Diet

This chapter is about getting started on the ketogenic diet. We have written it from the perspectives of each of the key parties who will be involved in initiating the diet because each one plays a different but important role:

- the parents, child, and family;
- the dietitian;
- the physician.

Starting the ketogenic diet will not be a rose garden. Minor obstacles will inevitably pop up. These bumps in the road are to be expected as a child progresses from many seizures to few seizures, ideally becoming completely seizure-free.

Getting started is the most difficult part. This is a time when, if they do not accept the challenge and overcome the obstacles, all parties involved may be tempted to throw up their hands and give in, even before the diet has a reasonable chance to succeed.

That is why we ask for a commitment of one to two months from a family before we recommend the diet. This time frame gives everyone a chance to overcome the initial bumps and correct any errors or misunderstandings that may arise when taking on a treatment as comprehensive as the ketogenic diet. At least one month is needed to see if indeed the benefits of the diet will outweigh its burdens.

GETTING READY FOR THE DIET: THE PARENTS' PERSPECTIVE

PSYCHOLOGICAL PREPARATION

The first, most important factor contributing to the success of the diet is the psychological factor. It is adopting the belief that the diet *will work*. It is the determination to get a child out of that medication haze, to stop those frustrating absences, to throw away the helmet that had to be worn as protection against drops.

If the parents start out as doubters, they will focus on the inevitable problems instead of appreciating the decrease in seizures and improved behavior of the child. It will be too much to bear when the child accidentally uses the wrong toothpaste, acts irritable and demanding, or gets sick and has a seizure three weeks into the treatment. It will be too sad when the child cries for afternoon cookies or Sunday night pizza.

If parents start out thinking positively, saying, "we will do whatever is necessary to give this diet a chance to work; the sacrifice is worthwhile if our child has a chance to become seizure-free," they are already halfway there.

Sometimes problems may not come from the parents. They may come from a "How-will-my-grandchild-know-it's-me-if-I-don't-bring-Hershey's-Kisses?" Grandma or a jealous "How-come-Peter-gets-all-the-attention?" sister. The optimism and faith that will carry a family through the diet (pardon us if this sounds a bit preachy) has to come from a team

> At first you're going to be afraid of temptation. You're going to feel bad about your child seeing others eat food he can't have. You'll be worried about what the diet's emotional effects will be. And you're going to be worried about whether your kid will cooperate. But you can live through it! If you have other kids, they can eat other foods. Try to be positive. The main thing to remember is, if the diet works your kid will be so happy to feel well again!
>
> —CC

effort, encompassing the whole family, especially the child. Once the diet is effective, once the seizures are controlled and the child is functioning better, it is much easier to maintain the momentum. At the start it can be very tough. It is the willingness of the parents to meet the challenge that will carry the family through.

GETTING THE CHILD'S COOPERATION

Children should be enlisted, rather than ordered, to participate in the diet. Children do not like having seizures. They do not like being different from their friends or taking medications. They want to be cured. If possible, explain to a child in an age-appropriate fashion how the diet may help fix these problems. If parents communicate their own enthusiasm, most children will buy in.

But no one should make promises that cannot be kept! Parents cannot guarantee that the seizures will disappear completely or that there will be no more medication. These are goals, but they cannot be promises.

The responsibility for sticking to the diet is ultimately the child's, so parents can help by giving children the psychological and emotional power to handle the tough parts. Role-playing may be useful. Parents can try rehearsing what to say in difficult situations. For instance, a parent might pretend to be a teacher offering a cracker at snack time, and let a child practice saying, "That's not on my diet, thank you!" Or a parent might pretend to be a friend trying to swap a sandwich for cheesecake at lunch, and teach the child responses such as, "No, I'm on a magic diet, I have to eat my own food."

Older children often need someone on whom they can vent their anger and frustrations. It is far better if this can be someone other than their parents. For teens and preteens we have sometimes set up special telephone times when they can call and talk to a counselor. It often starts with a weekly call, then becomes less frequent. Through these calls children can report successes and discuss problems, receive reinforcement, and hear stories about others who went through the same thing they did.

One of our counselor's favorite lines, when things seem particularly bleak and a child wants to quit the diet, is "Hey, it's up to you. No one is making you stay on the diet. You are always free to choose to stop— to go back to having seizures and taking medicine. It's all up to you." Putting the responsibility back on the child eliminates the parents and the counselor as bad guys and empowers the child to see the reality that if the diet is indeed working, the choices are really very simple.

> I told Michael, "It's your problem and you have to solve it. We are here to help you, but most of the work is going to be yours. You're a big guy, you can handle it." Michael is six, and he has never cheated once.
>
> —EH

Special Equipment

The only essential pieces of equipment needed for the ketogenic diet are a gram scale and a kit to test ketones in the urine. Parents must either buy a gram scale or make sure that the hospital plans to supply one the family can take home. The gram scale is the main calculating tool for the diet, so it is extremely important. At Johns Hopkins we make a gram scale available to parents at cost. Providing this service ensures that all parents get an accurate scale while saving them the time and effort of searching for one themselves. The scale should be accurate and should display weights in one gram increments.

Scales can be obtained through the postal department of most office supply stores. Electronic digital scales, although slightly more expensive, hold up better under the rigors of constant use and travel.

PELOUZE currently makes an electronic postal scale with one gram accuracy. Model PS2RIP. List price $160.00

PELOUZE will also be coming out with a digital food service scale with one gram accuracy. Anticipated manufacture date is April 1996. Model FS2.

OHAUS Corporation also manufactures a portable electronic scale with one gram accuracy, battery with AC adapter, Model LS 1200. These scales can only be obtained through a contract with a wholesale distributor. Interested hospitals or organizations can contact OHAUS Corporation at 29 Hanover Road, Florham Park, NJ 07932 (201) 377-9000.

Kits for testing ketone levels in the urine are commonly available in drugstores, often combined with glucose tests used by diabetics. Keto Diastix, manufactured by the Ames Company, is one such test kit.

Parents have found various equipment helpful while their children were on the ketogenic diet. The following is a long list gathered from several parents—it is meant as a source of ideas. All of this equipment is optional; parents may buy these supplies if and as needed:

- large collection of small plastic storage containers (such as Tupperware) or margarine tubs;
- screw-top plastic beverage containers;
- small rubber spatulas to be used as plate-cleaners;
- one-, two-, four-, and six-ounce plastic cups;
- a measuring cup marked with milliliters or a graduated cylinder for weighing and measuring;
- six or more Pyrex custard dishes for microwave cooking and freezing meals;
- popsicle molds;
- six-inch nonstick skillet for sautéeing individual portions with easy cleanup;
- travel cooler and/or an insulated bag;
- one or two small Thermoses for school and travel;
- toothpicks for picking up morsels of food to make eating fun;
- blender;
- milkshake wand or small hand beater;
- portable dual-burner electric camping stove for trips;
- masking tape for labels;
- bendable straws for drinking every drop;
- microwave oven.

To repeat, it is not necessary to own a lot of equipment before starting the diet: this is simply a sample list from various parents. The only supplies that are absolutely necessary prior to starting the diet, and may be purchased or obtained from the hospital, are a gram scale and a kit for testing ketone levels in urine.

SPECIAL FOODS

The only essential research parents need to do before starting the diet is to find out whether their neighborhood cream supply is 36 percent

Brian's mother called to report that he had eaten candy bars on Halloween. Since starting the diet he wasn't having any seizures for the first time in years, and she was concerned. I told her that if Brian wanted to call us we would be happy to talk to him, and we wouldn't tell him that his mother had called first.

So Brian called and started telling me about how hard and boring the diet was. I talked about how well I had heard he was doing in school. Eventually he told me about Halloween. I didn't yell like his father had, but talked instead about what a phenomenal job he had done for the last six months. I told him he was lucky nothing happened when he ate the candy, but that I was sure if he kept eating forbidden things the diet would not work and he would be right back where he started. "You have worked so hard and done so well, it would be a shame to lose that now," I told him. Brian is still on the diet, doing well, and not cheating. Being seizure-free should be a powerful reward for the child.

—DP

fat, 40 percent fat, or somewhere in between. The fat content of cream varies from one location to another. The content of available cream will affect the calculation of the diet, so it is important to find out what is available in a given neighborhood and to tell the dietitian before the child's diet is calculated.

Cream must be at least 36%, but may be as high as 40%. Plans are calculated the same. The 40% may have some additional fat, but will certainly not affect ketosis.

- To determine if the cream is correct, there should be 5.5 or 6 grams of total fat in a 15 ml serving. If there is any doubt at all, call the dairy directly. They are required by law to know the percentage on cream dispensed.
- Check to be sure that the cream does not contain added sugars such as dextrose.
- Once you find an acceptable brand, stick with it.

Other foods and flavorings that many parents have used to make the diet more fun for kids include:

- baking chocolate;
- fruit-flavored sugar-free diet soda such as Faygo;
- pure flavoring extracts: vanilla, almond, lemon, maple, coconut, chocolate;
- sugar-free flavored gelatin such as D-Zerta, Jell-O, or Royal;
- nonstick spray such as Pam or Mazola No-stick for cooking;
- calorie-free sweeteners such as Saccharine, Sweetest, Sucaryl, and liquid Sweet-10.

This list, like the equipment list, is intended as a source of ideas, not a must-buy-right-away order. The rest of the diet ingredients should be pure, fresh, simple foods—lean meat, fish, or poultry, bacon, eggs, cheese, fruit, vegetables, butter, mayonnaise, canola or olive oil.

• •

IMPORTANT

It is best to stick with the artificial sweeteners listed. Other sweeteners, such as Equal® (the blue stuff), Sweet 'N Low®(the pink stuff), and NutraSweet®, contain carbohydrates that can upset ketosis. Beware of any foods or medicines containing carbohydrates, including mannitol, sorbitol, dextrin, and many ingredients ending in "ose," such as maltose, lactose, fructose, glucose, sucrose, dextrose, or polycose. Many foods, candies, and gums billed as sugar-free are not carbohydrate-free and cannot be used on the diet.

• •

MEDICATIONS

Medications play an important role in the ultimate success of the ketogenic diet. Starches and sugars are frequently used as fillers and taste enhancers in all forms of medication—tablets, capsules, and liquids. These starches and sugars can easily be overlooked in diet formulation, but they can impair a child's ability to maintain high levels of ketosis. Read the labels of all medications carefully.

Also take into account carbohydrate contents of all medications, whether routine medications taken daily or intermittent medications given to treat conditions such as colds or infection. Ideally, the total carbohydrate content in medications should be less than .1 g. (or 100 mg.) for the entire day. Anything higher should be calculated into the meal plan's daily carbohydrate allotment. For example, a child taking .09 g. (90 mg.) of phenobarbital at bedtime in the form of three .03 g. (30 mg.) tablets receives .07 g. (72 mg.) of starch and lactose per tablet, or a daily total of .21 g. (216 mg.). Some of the new anticonvulsants do not come in sugar-free form. If they must be continued, the carbohydrate content should be calculated in the diet. During the starvation and diet initiation phase, the carbohydrate can be ignored.

Difficulty in prescribing medications for a child on the ketogenic diet often arises from the fact that many common over-the-counter and prescription medications are not available in a sugar-free form. Many of those that are listed as "sugar-free" in references are appropriate for use in the diabetic population but not for children on the ketogenic diet. Frequently, medications listed as sugar-free contain starch in sugar substitutes such as sorbitol and mannitol. The Food and Drug Administration does not require the listing of inactive ingredients such as sorbitol in the labeling of oral prescription drugs, and even when ingredients are listed, their precise amounts are often not found on the label. Additionally, manufacturers frequently are reluctant to release information about the amounts of particular ingredients in a medication, contending that this is proprietary information or that formulations change frequently. They can usually be persuaded to release the information, however, if it is important for treatment of a specific patient.

A pharmacist who is willing to get to know the diet and the child and work with the family for the duration can be a valuable asset, helping to interpret labels and call manufacturers if necessary. Before starting the diet, a source of sugar-free and lactose-free multivitamins, such as MeadJohnson's Poly-Vi-Sol (liquid or drops) with iron or Ross's Vi-Daylin multivitamin with iron should be located, as well as 600 to 650 mg. calcium supplements such as Rugby's calcium gluconate, and toothpaste (Tom's Natural, Arm & Hammer, and Ultra brite are allowed). Routine medications that are taken daily should come from a single laboratory, as ingredient concentrations vary among manufacturers.

General rules for the use of medications, a selected list of medications that have been used by children on the diet, and contact information for pharmaceutical manufacturers can be found in Appendix A at the back of this book.

PREPARING FOR ADMISSION

The hospital stay is typically three to five days. People often ask why a child has to be hospitalized while starting the diet. The reasons are that in the hospital:

- physicians can supervise the fasting and guard against potentially serious symptoms of hypoglycemia;
- physicians can adjust medication levels according to the child's needs; we often reduce one or more medications to avoid the toxicity induced with the acidosis and ketosis;
- dietitians can meet intensively with parents and train them to prepare the diet.

IDEAL HOSPITALIZATION SCHEDULE

Day 0: Child eats no carbohydrates or sweets.
Parents meet with dietitian to learn about diet theory.
Child begins to fast after dinner.

Day 1: Admission to hospital.
Fasting continues.
Liquids are limited to 60 to 70 cc/kg of body weight.
Parents meet with dietitian to discuss food preferences.

Day 2: Child begins to register elevated urinary ketones.
Dietitian calculates meal plans.
Parents start learning how to plan and prepare diet.

Day 3: Child, in ketosis, starts food with one-third strength meals.
Parents learn to use scales and prepare meals with dietitian's assistance.

Day 4: Child progresses to two-thirds strength meals. Dietitian completes child's meal plans and basic training with parents.

Day 5: Child starts full diet and is discharged from hospital if all is going well.

One day prior to admission, parents are requested to eliminate sweets and carbohydrates (bread, rice, cereal, potatoes, noodles) from the child's food. The child can eat as much protein (meat, chicken, cheese, eggs), vegetables, fruit, and fat as desired. No solid food should be eaten after dinner.

Cutting out sweets and carbohydrates a day in advance of admission, and fasting on the day of admission, will shorten the amount of time the child has to spend in the hospital as well as the fasting period before the first ketogenic meals can begin. It is often difficult for parents to watch a child fasting; a parent's instinct is to feed a child. Some children vomit or become listless while fasting, and some have a temporary upward swing in seizure activity before the benefits of the diet begin to show. This is difficult for parents to watch. Indeed, many parents say that the fasting stage of the diet is harder on them than on the child.

Both parents should be present on the day of admission if possible. In addition to being a day on which a child will need a great deal of support, this is the day the parents will meet the dietitian and begin learning about the theory and practice of the diet. At least one parent should remain with the child for the duration of the hospital stay.

During your child's hospital admission, be aware that the following commonly occur and are not setbacks to starting the diet:

- Low blood sugar. As your child continues his/her fast, the blood sugar will gradually decrease. Children frequently become very sleepy during this time and prefer to rest or engage in quiet activities. Energy levels may take up to 1–2 weeks to return to normal.

- Medication toxicity. Drug levels frequently go up even though there has been no change in dosage once the fasting has begun. This increase may be enough to cause toxicity. If that happens, the dosage should be reduced.

- Seizure activity may increase, decrease, or stay the same. Some children demonstrate a dramatic improvement in seizure activity once ketosis is reached. This is a very positive sign and indicates that the diet may ultimately be helpful in controlling seizures. Some children show an increase in activity—possibly due to the stress of admission and drastic changes in routine, lack of sleep, and/or medication toxicity., Parents should not get discouraged. Seizures usually decrease once the children are adjusted to the diet and normalized back into their own environment.

- Refusal to eat—ketosis, low blood sugar, and energy levels, and lack of solid food can greatly decrease your child's appetite. Initial meals are only one-third of total quantities and are usually accepted without difficulty. If your child does refuse to eat, encourage him or her to eat as much as possible. A positive approach is essential! What is not eaten in twenty to thirty minutes should be thrown away without a fuss. Even very young children can sense the new focus that is being placed on what and when they eat. If parents allow this to become a source of battle right from the beginning, it will be a very long two to three years on the diet. Some of this problem can be avoided by encouraging plenty of fluids during the fast.

Insurance companies are usually willing to pay for the five day hospital stay once they understand what the diet is, the reasons for hospitalization, and the fact that it will ultimately save them money. A sample explanatory letter that we send to insurance companies is on page 93.

THE DIETITIAN'S PERSPECTIVE

PREPARING THE HOSPITAL STAFF

The dietitian supervising the ketogenic diet has traditionally been the leader of the treatment as practiced at Johns Hopkins. We use the term *dietitian*, but specifically trained nurses, and even parents, have assumed the lead role in calculating the diet and training others in the proper use of the ketogenic diet. Perhaps a more encompassing name might be the "ketocoach." In conjunction with the physician, the dietitian will be running the ketogenic diet protocol, starting with the hospitalization and continuing throughout the entire period that the child is on the diet, up to two to three years. The consulting dietitian is the captain leading the parents and child through the diet's shoals and rocks.

To initiate the diet, the dietitian assists the physician in writing the initial diet order, the fluid restriction order, and any other orders pertaining to the hospitalization. During the child's hospital stay, the dietitian keeps up to date on the reports and requests of the nurses and works with the dietary staff to coordinate the delivery and preparation of the proper ketogenic food. Prior to admission, the consulting dietitian will already have spoken to the parents, sent a nutrition history form, and obtained the information necessary to start calculating meal plans based on the family's habits and the child's restrictions and food preferences.

During the admission process, the supervising dietitian will be the one who sees the whole picture. The dietitian's responsibilities include:

- HOSPITAL PREPARATION. If the institution is not familiar with the diet, there will be a lot of work to do in preparation for an admission. Is the nutrition department ready and able to provide the proper food? Does the ward have gram scales and graduated cylinders for weighing and measuring the food? Are sugar-, lactose-, and carbohydrate-free toothpaste and medications available in the pharmacy? Does the hospital stock 36 percent or 40 percent cream, or does that have to be special ordered ahead of time? Are sugar-free, decaffeinated beverages available? If the institution has done the diet previously, the supervising dietitian still has to keep on top of the situation to see that all necessities are available and that ever-changing new staff members are properly trained.
- STAFF TRAINING. Nurses, nutrition staff, and attending physicians will need in-service training in the ketogenic diet protocol. The dietitian will teach nurses to be responsible for:
  - monitoring the child's food and beverage intake according to the diet order;
  - preventing the child from obtaining extra food on the ward;
  - monitoring blood glucose and medication levels;
  - monitoring urinary ketone levels;
  - ensuring that medications, toothpaste, etc. are sugar-free;
  - recognizing when hypoglycemia is merely transient and when it is serious, requiring immediate attention;

◆ being alert to the order to start feeding and the progression of the diet from one-third to two-thirds to full quantity;
◆ informing the dietitian or physician of any problems or special circumstances that arise with the child or family.

At the same time, the dietitian will teach the dietitian's assistant or nutrition staff to be responsible for:

◆ ordering food from the main kitchen and then weighing and measuring the proper quantities of food according to the diet order for each individual meal;
◆ having gram scales and graduated cylinders on hand, as well as vanilla, saccharin, a hand beater, tartar sauce, catsup, a can of tuna, or other items that might help make hospital food palatable;
◆ assisting the dietitian in teaching the parents to weigh and prepare the meals;
◆ double-checking the dietitian's calculations and meal plans for possible mistakes;
◆ checking with the supervising dietitian about any requests for extra food or food changes;
◆ notifying the dietitian of any emergency admissions;
◆ notifying the dietitian if the family is having any problems with the ketogenic diet protocol;

All hospital staff should clearly understand that the child is to be allowed nothing but allotted amounts of noncaloric liquids (water, herbal tea, or decaffeinated diet soda) during the fast, and later only the exact food prescribed on the meal plan.

• COACHING PARENTS. While the child is in the hospital, training the parents to prepare the diet at home is obviously one of the dietitian's major tasks. As mentioned previously, the dietitian usually meets or communicates with the parents even before the patient is admitted. The process of communicating with the family while the child is in the hospital is discussed below.

It is extremely important that the supervising dietitian stay on top of the hospital routine and make all those involved in providing food and medications to the child in the hospital aware of the child's special needs.

COMMUNICATING WITH THE FAMILY

The time that the child spends in the hospital provides an opportunity for the dietitian to train the parents in planning and preparing the meals. Indeed, intensive training of parents during daily meetings is one of the primary reasons for the hospital stay. This is the dietitian's chance to instill faith, give support, and get the family started on the right foot, equipped with knowledge and a can-do attitude.

As soon as the family reaches the hospital, the dietitian should meet with the parents. The purpose of this meeting is to:

- learn about the child's eating habits and home life by taking a good nutrition history so that individualized meal plans can be calculated, or meal plans that were devised based on preliminary communications prior to admission can be refined;
- begin teaching the parents about the theory and principles of the diet;
- answer any questions, allay the parents' fears, and get them thinking positively about the diet as a road to relief from seizures

The nutrition history and food preference form shown in Figure 6 is adapted from forms we have used for many years. The parents' input and the dietitian's impression of the child's habits gained from the preliminary meeting will be helpful in devising meal plans that make the diet as easy as possible for both parents and child. The dietitian should ask the parents about all aspects of home life as they relate to eating habits:

- Who normally takes care of the child?
- Who does the shopping and cooking?
- Are there other siblings? If so, how many and how old?
- Do the parents work? What is their schedule?
- What is a typical breakfast, lunch, and dinner?
- Does the child attend school or day care? Carry lunch or eat at home?

FIGURE 6   KETOGENIC DIET

NUTRITION HISTORY AND FOOD PREFERENCES

Name _____ Age _____ M _____ F _____ Height _____

Parents' Names _____ Usual Weight _____ Weight Change? _____

Address _____

Medications _____

_____

Phone (H) _____ Special Needs _____

Phone (O) _____ Bowels N C D   Appetite S M L

MEAL	TIME	AVERAGE MENUS	COMMENTS
Breakfast	_____		
Lunch	_____		
Dinner	_____		
Snacks	_____		

FAVORITE BEVERAGES (circle):   Water   Soda   Milk   Iced/Hot Tea

Orange/Apple Juice   Cold/Hot Chocolate   Lemonade   Chocolate/Vanilla Milkshake

Coffee   Other:_____

LIKES (circle):   Peanut Butter   Cottage Cheese   Cream Cheese   Bacon

Butter   Mayonnaise

MORE Likes (Dairy/Meat/Fruit/Vegetable): _____

Notes: _____

_____

- Is the child a big eater? A picky eater?
- Is this a one-parent home? Do relatives or grandparents play a large role in family life?

The better the dietitian can fit the meal plans to the family's eating habits, the greater the chance that the family will make the diet work. Getting a picture of the family's home life also makes analyzing any future difficulties with the diet easier.

Teaching the parents about the principles of the diet helps them to better understand why it must be followed so strictly, and what changes or substitutions are reasonable. The more parents know, the easier the dietitian's job will be. When the parents come into the hospital, give them a crash course. Explain what ketones are, the purpose of fasting, and what is known about how the diet functions. Much of this information is contained in Chapters 1 and 3 of this book.

Parents should also have a chance to discuss their questions and fears with you soon after they arrive at the hospital to make them more comfortable with the diet. Emphasize that the reason they are trying the diet is to control seizures and improve the quality of their life as well as that of their child. They should always try to keep those benefits in mind, even if the diet gets tough.

Parents can often get exceptional support by talking with other parents who have been through the diet. Soon after the diet is suggested for their child, perhaps even before the hospital stay, they should be encouraged to contact other parents of children who have been or are currently on the diet, especially those living nearby. Old-timers are often pleased to speak with newcomers, to share advice and information and help them understand what to expect.

• •

D O N ' T   F O R G E T !

All children must take sugarless multivitamin and calcium supplements every day!

• •

PREPARING THE MEAL PLANS

Most children will be started on a 4:1 ratio. Since infants have proportionately more body fat, they have a tendency to burn body fat to make sugar and seem to have less tolerance of a 4:1 ratio, so we sometimes start them on 3:1. Teens need more protein and are also often started on 3:1.

By the time the child is ready to start eating, a reasonable number of basic meal plans should be prepared for use during the hospital stay and for the parents to take home. When working up the meal plans, the dietitian should try to imagine the needs of the child and the parents, or whoever will be preparing the meals. Does the child love butter? Hate eggs? Go to school? Like hot lunches? Prefer soft food or crunchy food? Aside from faith and commitment on the part of the parents, making the diet as close as possible to the child's usual food preferences is one of the most important factors for success.

Traditionally, as mentioned in Chapter 4, the basic meal plans have been given to the parents in generic form:

1. Meat/fish/poultry, fruit, fat, cream.
2. Cheese, fruit, fat, cream.
3. Egg, fruit, fat, cream.
4. Meat/fish/poultry, vegetables, fat, cream.
5. Cheese, vegetables, fat, cream.
6. Egg, vegetables, fat, cream.

It has then been up to the parents (with the dietitian's help at first) to learn how to translate generic meal plans into real food. The basic meals above correspond to the following menus:

1. Chicken cutlet with butter, strawberry whipped cream parfait.
2. Cheese rolls with mayonnaise, peach slices, popsicle.
3. Scrambled egg, butter, orange juice, diluted cream.
4. Sliced hot dog, buttered sauerkraut, vanilla ice cream.
5. Asparagus cheese melt, lettuce leaf with mayonnaise, coconut cream.
6. Mushroom omelette with butter, cream-Faygo whip.

Most children are satisfied with a limited variety of favorite foods. One parent prepared mushroom omelettes every meal for one week until she had enough courage to try a second meal plan. Her six-year-old was very happy.

When calculating the meal plans by hand, the dietitian must check and recheck the numbers, as the success of the child's treatment depends on the accuracy of the calculation. The computer program now available is designed to make the calculations and menu planning easier. It has many meal plans in its database. The procedure used to calculate the proper allotments of calories, protein, fat, and carbohydrates as well as devise individual meal plans is detailed in Chapter 9.

Approximately twenty-four to forty-eight hours of fasting are necessary before a child reaches deep ketosis and is ready to eat the first meal. If the dietitian does not have time right away to calculate eighteen to twenty-four meal plans that are needed for home use, the six basic meal plans can ensure that once the physician decides that feeding should begin, the child's first meal will not be delayed.

• •

When using the hand-calculation method, all meal plans should be calculated with 10 percent fruit and Group B vegetables. Parents can then double the volume when they use Group A vegetables and use two-thirds of the amount prescribed if they choose 15 percent fruit, using the exchange lists given in Chapter 4.

• •

EGGNOG AND HOSPITAL FOOD

Coaxing a palatable first meal out of a hospital kitchen can be nearly impossible. The first meal of only one-third quantity can be particularly dismaying unless extra care is taken to make it attractive, and a hospital is rarely equipped to provide attractive customized meals. At Johns Hopkins, therefore, we sometimes feed a child ketogenic eggnog for the two days of the hospital stay, beginning with one-third of the full diet quantity for the first three meals, and two-thirds for the second three meals. When the full quantity is reached, real food may be served, or the child may again be given eggnog. Ketogenic eggnog is the only meal that does not need to be eaten all at once, so a child sipping eggnog will not be under as much pressure as one faced with a plate of unfamiliar food. At home the parent can prepare more appetizing, familiar meals. If eggnog is served at the hospital instead of solid food, however, it is important that parents be given enough training in preparing solid food meals so that they will be able to do it comfortably at home.

In some states raw eggs cannot be used in the preparation of hospital food. In this situation, some centers have chosen to use sterilized or frozen eggs. Another option is the use of an egg substitute. Land O' Lakes Country Morning best approximates real eggs in terms of fat, protein, and carbohydrate. There are many other egg substitutes on the market, but many of them are low in fat and inappropriate for the ketogenic diet.

TRAINING THE PARENTS

When the child's meal plans are ready, the parents should be assigned the job of writing down a week's worth of detailed breakfast, lunch, and dinner menus for use at home. This encourages parents to stretch their imagination and become ready for cooking the diet. It is also a good teaching tool, allowing the dietitian to go over these menus with the parents, making corrections or adjustments if necessary.

While the parents are in the hospital, the supervising dietitian should meet with them each day. The parents must learn to:

- understand the principles of the diet;
- use a gram scale;
- create actual menus from generic meal plans;
- prepare attractive and palatable meals at home.

The child's meals in the hospital, whether eggnog or solid food, may be used as a lesson. The supervising dietitian or the nutrition assistants on the ward can invite the parents to watch or participate as meals are weighed on the gram scale and assembled from a calculated meal plan using ingredients that have been ordered from the hospital kitchen.

As long as the child is in the hospital, close work must be continued with the hospital nutrition staff to make sure that meals are ordered once feeding starts, foods are weighed properly, and the child is provided three appropriate meals each day.

THE PHYSICIAN'S PERSPECTIVE

Initiating the ketogenic diet may seem simple from a medical perspective but in our experience at Johns Hopkins we have seen that Murphy's Law often prevails—anything that can go wrong will go wrong. The health care team must be thinking at all times, keeping lines of communication open, keeping the goals of the diet in mind, and using good clinical judgment. Remember, clinical judgment is a precious commodity to be used, not saved.

> Jane was brought into the hospital for initiation of the diet. Since she was small, the intern started an IV, explaining that it was "just in case she needs glucose." After two days of starvation, Jane was still not in ketosis. Guess what was found in her IV—glucose!
>
> —JF

FASTING: THE MOST CRITICAL PERIOD

After the child is admitted to the hospital, no food and only limited amounts of water, herbal tea, or decaffeinated diet beverage are allowed (approximately 60–70 cc. liquid per kilogram of body weight, or about one cc. for each calorie on the diet). If the child still feels thirsty after finishing the liquid allotment, a small cup of ice chips may be provided to chew on. It is best to divide the allotted liquid into small amounts of no more than 120 cc. given at one- to two-hour intervals.

The physician must write an order for fasting and restricted fluid intake in the child's medical chart. The fast normally lasts approximately two days. During this time blood sugar should be closely watched, particularly in smaller children. The physician should be alert for symptomatic hypoglycemia and should watch and adjust medications if necessary, as discussed below. But if everything is going well, very little medical treatment should be required.

In these cost-conscious times, some students and residents (not to mention insurance companies) have asked why a child is hospitalized if medical treatment during the hospitalization is usually so minimal. To these people we explain that there is nothing minimal about the ketogenic diet—changing the body's basic metabolism is quite radical. In any case, close medical supervision in a hospital context is essential for those cases in which everything does not go well—for instance, in the case of hypoglycemia, medication toxicity, or an excess of ketosis.

WHAT CAN GO WRONG DURING THE FAST?

FAILURE TO GO INTO KETOSIS

If ketosis is not developing as it should, the problem is likely to be logistical. Recheck everything. Was an IV hooked up? If so, why? Is there glucose in the IV? Is the child still receiving any medications in forms that contain sugar or carbohydrates? Is the child using the proper sugarless toothpaste? Did the nurses inadvertently feed the child or allow the child to wander into rooms where food was available? Was the child sedated for a test, and was sleepiness then mistaken for hypoglycemia for which orange juice was given? We have seen all these problems and more.

As discussed previously, infants under twenty-four months may have a more difficult time getting into full ketosis—and are more prone to hypoglycemia. If after forty-eight hours, they are still not in 4+ ketosis, feeding may begin. Ultimately, deeper ketosis will be achieved as the diet progresses. Older children, however, should fast until full ketosis is reached, regardless of the time. Starting to feed too early may make fine-tuning more difficult later.

HYPOGLYCEMIA

During the fast the child's medical condition should be closely watched. Blood sugar should be checked every four to six hours. Medication levels should be checked daily or if the child becomes

too sleepy. Urine should be checked two to three times a day for acetone and diacetic acid, or ketone levels. Blood and urine charts should
be kept up to date.

Often a child's blood sugar falls to relatively low levels (around 40
mg. per 100 cc.) but children usually show no signs of hypoglycemia
at that level. If there are no other symptoms of hypoglycemia, no action
is needed other than continued supervision to ensure that the problem
corrects itself or that the child does not develop symptoms.

> Roger had his blood sugar checked every four hours. When
> it fell to 40 mg% the resident gave him 60 cc. of orange
> juice. Four hours later the blood sugar had again fallen to
> 37 mg% and he was given 60 cc. of juice. After two days of
> fasting Roger was not ketotic—guess why? Right! The sugar
> in the juice was preventing it!
>
> "Why was I supposed to test for low blood sugar if I
> wasn't going to treat it?" asked the resident who gave Roger
> the juice. He was not using his clinical judgment to tell the
> difference between a potentially dangerous hypoglycemia
> and a normal, transient side effect of fasting—and he was
> casually giving juice that prevented ketosis, the primary
> purpose for Roger's hospital stay.
>
> —JF

The symptoms of hypoglycemia are:

- paleness;
- sweaty forehead;
- excess sleep;
- rapid pulse;
- dizziness;
- nausea.

HYPOGLYCEMIA: A CHECKLIST

◆ If the blood sugar is 30 to 40 mg% and the child appears well, watch closely. Recheck the sugar in two hours. If the child otherwise looks OK, do nothing.

◆ If the sugar drops below 25 mg%, watch the child very closely. If it is an older child and there are no symptoms, do nothing but continue to watch.

◆ If a younger child has sugar as low as 25 mg%, watch very, very carefully for symptoms of serious hypoglycemia.

◆ If symptoms of hypoglycemia do occur—if a child feels nauseous, is weak, sweating profusely, dizzy, pale, or very sleepy—15–30 cc. of orange juice should be given. The child may also be given a cup of cracked ice to chew on. If juice does not stop the nausea at first, another 15 cc. may be given in an hour. Too much juice will delay or prevent onset of ketosis.

◆ If the young child's blood sugar falls below 25 mg%, even without symptoms, 30 cc. of orange juice should be given. Check the blood sugar again in an hour and give another 30 cc. of orange juice if necessary.

◆ If a child has seizures or major changes in consciousness and the blood sugar drops below 25 mg%, a 5% dextrose solution should be given intravenously immediately.

A low blood sugar is not uncommon with fasting. A very low sugar, one that causes symptoms, is very uncommon, especially in older children, but it could be serious. That is why blood sugar must be tracked every four to six hours during the fasting phase. To repeat: if the hypoglycemia is not symptomatic, there is no need to treat it.

●●

IF POSSIBLE, AVOID TESTS REQUIRING SEDATION

If possible, schedule tests that require sedation, such as electroencepha-lograms (EEGs) and scans, before admitting the child for starvation. It is difficult to separate the sleepiness and irritability of the sedation used for the tests from the effects of hypoglycemia. This can lead to unnecessary concern over a child's health while fasting.

●●

EXCESS KETOSIS

Another potential problem that can arise during a fast is an excess of ketosis, which can lead to nausea, excess sleepiness, Kussmaul's breath-ing, and sometimes vomiting. If a child is very nauseous during the fast, or if refusal to eat the meals after the fast appears to be due to excess ketosis, we give 30–60 cc. of orange juice, sometimes with a teaspoon of sugar mixed in. This can break up the ketosis slightly and help the child get ready to start eating the ketogenic meals. Inadequate fluid intake may also lead to sedation and vomiting. If the child is far behind in fluid intake, IV fluid (without sugar) may be needed.

Q: What should I do if I am not sure whether or not the child's symptoms are due to blood sugar levels?

A: If the child has symptoms that might be caused by hypoglycemia but might also be a result of other factors—for instance, the child is sleepy and irritable but it is the middle of the night, or medication lev-els have not been reduced, or the child was sedated for a test—and the blood sugar is low, give a small amount of orange juice or glucose if you are concerned. It is better to give a small amount of glucose or orange juice when in doubt than to suffer the effects of hypoglycemia. But if glucose is given too often, the child will never achieve ketosis.

Q: What if the child is sleepy and irritable, but the blood sugar is not dangerously low?

A: If sleepiness is the primary symptom, check whether medications have been reduced. We generally cut at least one of the sedating med-

THE CASE OF EDGAR

Edgar is a roly-poly four-year-old who is fed by nasogastric tube because of profound neurologic damage. After two days of starvation he still only has small amounts of ketones in the urine.

WHAT COULD BE THE MATTER WITH EDGAR?

- Perhaps Edgar has enough energy stores that he is still burning them completely after two days. Remember, ketones are the result of incompletely burned glucose or fats.
- Perhaps Edgar is actually ketotic, but is getting too much fluid. The same amount of ketones measure as "low" in diluted urine, but "high" in concentrated urine.
- Urinary ketones are lower in the morning than in the evening, so check the time the ketones are being measured.

WHAT SHOULD BE DONE ABOUT EDGAR?

- After two days you should probably start the feeding with one-third of the diet even without high ketones. If the diet is properly calculated, Edgar should become progressively ketotic as the diet is implemented.

—JF

ications—phenobarbital or benzodiazepine—in half at the start of fasting and eliminate it with the start of feeding, as discussed below. Sleepiness can also be caused by sedation from a test or by an excess of ketosis.

THE FIRST MEAL

The children will be ready to begin eating when the urine shows a four-plus acetone (ketone) level. Traditionally, children fasted until they had lost 10 percent of their body weight before beginning the diet. They were also required to have a four-plus diacetic acid level, a urine specific gravity of 1.020 to 1.025, and a blood CO_2 between 10 and 12 mg/liter. We no longer rigidly follow this, as the benefits of the weight loss and other documentation of severe ketoacidosis are unclear. A four-plus level of ketones in the urine is now thought to be a sufficient criterion for eating to begin after the fast. Indeed, a two-day fast alone may be sufficient, as illustrated by the case of Edgar.

When sufficient ketosis is achieved, the physician should write an order to start feeding and make sure that the dietitian is aware of this decision so that food can be ordered in time for the next meal. The food order should indicate the calorie level, ketogenic ratio, and grams of protein, carbohydrate, and fat.

We generally begin feeding with one-third of the total calories for the first three meals after fasting, progress to two-thirds of the total calories for meals four, five, and six, and then progress to the full diet quantity. The child is discharged from the hospital after having at least one or two meals of the full diet. The rationale for this is that if children who were hungry from a fast wolfed down the full-quantity meal right away, they might vomit. There also is occasional difficulty in adapting to the high fat content of the food, resulting in nausea, vomiting, or diarrhea. A gradual introduction to ketogenic meals is thus considered prudent.

We have found that initiating feeding with one-third of the calculated eggnog for meals 1, 2, and 3, and two-thirds for the next three meals, is an efficient way to bypass the problem of in-hospital meals.

WHAT CAN GO WRONG WITH THE FIRST MEALS?

REFUSING FOOD

One of the basic rules of the ketogenic diet is that all food must be eaten at every meal, but sometimes children refuse to eat all the food in the first meal, or refuse to drink the cream. They are supposed to be hungry enough from fasting that anything looks tasty, but hospital food is . . .

well, it's famous for being that way, and cream is something kids are not used to drinking anyway. If this problem arises, the child should be coaxed—not bullied or ordered, but coaxed—into eating. Don't try a test of wills; children usually win. The diet can work only if it is accepted by both parents and child.

Sometimes a child can be encouraged to eat by mixing the cream with allotted diet soda or freezing it as ice cream. The cream can be diluted with water or sweetened with a saccharin tablet. Food in the meal should have been ordered with the child's preferences in mind, but no one relishes hospital food! Encouraging the child to accept the food at the start is a good exercise for the parents in coping with the diet in the future. At home parents are able to cook things they know their child likes, so food refusal is less likely to be a problem. As an alternative, eggnog can be substituted for food during some or all of the hospital stay.

NAUSEA

Ketosis itself decreases the appetite and may cause nausea, especially during the first week. If the child is truly refusing food and liquid or is very nauseated, sometimes ketosis can be modified by giving 30–60 cc. of orange juice. The child will become less ketotic, but then may start eating again, and the diet can be resumed. Another possibility for nauseated children, in the hospital as well as at home, is to give them ketogenic eggnog (see Chapter 4 for the recipe). With the eggnog, every sip is ketogenically balanced, so it does not matter if the child drinks it all or only drinks a little at a time.

If the fasting has been well-tolerated, and the child is not too sleepy

When he was taken off the medication, it was as if a shade was pulled up that had been drawn over his mind. He was brighter and more alert immediately, with no seizures. I always knew he was a bright child, but now I think he might be really smart.

—EH

or dehydrated by the start of feeding, the child can probably be discharged even if there are problems with eating. At home the parents have more freedom to adapt the diet to the child's individual tastes.

Vomiting once or twice when meals are introduced is not uncommon.

Reducing Medications

If phenobarbital has been prescribed, it is usually either markedly decreased or stopped altogether after the fasting period begins. It is often cut in half at the onset of fasting and eliminated entirely when feeding begins. This is because the acidosis of starvation allows more phenobarbital to enter the brain and thus children can become very sleepy. Depending on what other medications the child is on, we often stop or reduce one other medication in addition to phenobarbital at the onset of the fasting period.

The remaining medications are generally left in place until it can be seen if the child is doing well on the diet. If the child is doing well and the seizures are gone, the other anticonvulsant medications can be tapered off one at a time over a period of several weeks. If in the early stages of the diet the child is listless, too sleepy, and apathetic, medications may need to be adjusted more rapidly. The goal, when possible, is for the child to become seizure-free and medication-free on the diet alone. But it is important not to adjust too many things at once.

Decreasing some medications in the hospital may also have substantial psychologic benefits for the family. They are "already seeing progress" and benefits from starting the diet.

Other Variations in the Diet

Changes in the diet prescription, such as an increase to a 5:1 ketogenic ratio or an adjustment in the allotted number of calories, should be made at separate times from changes in medication dosages so that the results of one change will not cloud those of the other. These and other fine-tunings are discussed in the next chapter.

WILL INSURANCE PAY FOR THE ADMISSION?

Approval of the admission by the insurance company must be given prior to admission. In our experience, insurance companies often are initially reluctant to accept the ketogenic diet as a treatment requiring several days of hospitalization. They challenge the need to be hospitalized to go on a diet. When we explain the diet, how it may save visits to the emergency room, save medication bills, and perhaps even cure the epilepsy, insurance companies become more receptive. One family documented $100,000 in medical bills for their child in the year before the diet, between emergency room visits, scans, hospitalization for status epilepticus, medications, and an operation. In the first six months after starting the diet, medical bills totaled $45. Talking about the risks of fasting also helps to get insurance companies' attention. The following is typical of the letter we send to insurance companies:

To Whom It May Concern:

_____ is a _____ -year-old child with a history of uncontrolled seizure disorder. His/her seizures remain quite intractable and are in fact worsening despite a trial at multiple medications, both singly and in combination. He/she has tried _____ , _____ , _____ , and _____ . In spite of all these pharmacological attempts, _____'s seizures remain out of control. We would like to try the ketogenic diet as a treatment for his/her uncontrolled seizure disorder.

The ketogenic diet is a rigid, mathematically calculated treatment that is an accepted mode of therapy for children with intractable seizures. This treatment has been in existence since the 1920s and is *not experimental*. It is a high fat, low carbohydrate, low protein diet designed to maintain the patient in a constant state of ketosis. It is the ketosis that serves to abate seizures. Many centers do not use the diet or are not familiar with it because of its rigidity and the commitment in knowledge and energy required on the part of the center to effectively implement it.

Induction of the diet involves a four-day hospital stay. During the first forty-eight hours the child is fasting to deplete carbohydrate stores and achieve ketosis. Hospitalization is necessary to closely monitor and treat low glucose levels, as well as medication toxicity. The high fat diet is then slowly introduced. Complications during this period include low glucose levels, nausea, vomiting, and diarrhea. Additionally, hospitalization provides time for extensive teaching and impresses upon the parents the seriousness of the diet. While the latter is not the foundation for why we choose to do this in-hospital, it helps insure success and commitment to the diet once the family goes home.

What we hope to achieve through use of the diet is a complete cessation of _____ 's seizures or at least a significant reduction and/or elimination of some of the medication he/she is on, thus making him/her more alert and increasing his/her potential for greater learning and development.

We will be able to admit _____ for the hospital stay on X/XX/XX with an out-patient EEG on X/XX/XX. The total cost of hospitalization will run about $_____ . This includes hospital room and board, professional fees, nutrition consultant fees for both the hospital stay and one year following discharge, and one out-patient EEG. We will also need to see _____ in clinic for follow-up at three months, six months, and one year (more frequently if _____ has significant problems). The cost of these visits is $_____ /visit plus laboratory fees at each visit and an out-patient EEG at six and twelve months.

If you have questions, or if I can be of further assistance, please do not hesitate to call my office at (xxx) XXX-XXXX.

Thank you for your consideration.

Sincerely,

_____

While insurance companies often initially challenge hospitalization for a ketogenic diet, they do usually accept the treatment when they understand the reasons for the diet and for hospitalization. In the future, it may be possible to initiate the diet as an outpatient procedure in well-supervised circumstances, such as a hotel or facility near a hospital coordinated with a program of frequent visits to an outpatient clinic, but we currently find it beneficial to all parties to hospitalize children in the process of initiating the diet.

THE PARENTS' PERSPECTIVE AGAIN

THE FIRST MEAL ("IS THAT ALL THERE IS?")

Be prepared for the reality of the first meal—it will be very small. The ketogenic diet in general provides less bulk than a normal diet, and the first meal is only one-third the quantity of a full ketogenic meal. In addition to being small, first meals will also be rather basic—hospitals are not usually set up to do fun things like make a vanilla milkshake out of the cream. Parents can try to talk with the dietitian to make the first hospital meal as palatable as possible.

The child can take as much time as desired to eat the hospital meals, but everything must be eaten in order to maintain ketosis. Any food that is not eaten will be taken away: it cannot be saved for the next meal or for an in-between meal snack. For all of these reasons, we now use the one-third and two-thirds eggnog for the meals of the first two days.

LEAVING THE HOSPITAL

When going home from the hospital, parents should be given a container of ketogenic eggnog to use in place of up to three meals. The eggnog will tide the child over during travel and give the parent time to make the necessary purchases and prepare the first solid ketogenic diet meal at home.

When children leave the hospital after starting the diet, they may feel shaky and weak for a few days. This is because:

- fasting has drained their energy;
- the diet provides less food and water than they are used to;
- their bodies are getting accustomed to burning fat instead of glucose for energy.

Within a few days, however, strength and normal fitness should return. This is often a difficult time for the whole family. There has been a lot to learn, it probably seems overwhelming, and the prospect for ultimate success of the diet is still uncertain. This is the time when the family must gather its strength and receive strong support from the physician and dietitian. This is when a ketocoach may be most helpful.

The doctor and dietitian need to bolster the parents' confidence even as the parents are bolstering the child's. This is a time for patience, hope, and positive thinking. If parents are concerned that their child looks weak and frail, they should be encouraged to wait a few days until the child has time to recover from the fast. If they worry that the child lacks energy while hospitalized or within the first few days of returning home, they should be encouraged to focus instead on whether the child has had fewer seizures than before or whether alertness has increased since the medications were reduced. If the child continues to have seizures, the parents must remember that it may take a few days, or weeks, to break the habits (and seizures) of the past. Before they came to the hospital, the family will have agreed to give the diet a one-month chance. If the diet is to be given its best chance to work, the family must persevere even if the first days or weeks are difficult.

The way the physician answers parents' early concerns and questions can determine the family's level of confidence and perseverance on the diet. The process of adapting to the diet at home is a separate topic, which is discussed at length in the next chapter.

DEVELOPING A SUCCESSFUL KETOGENIC DIET PROGRAM: THE ROLE OF A KETOCOACH

We have talked about the lead role of the dietitian in preparing the nursing staff of the floor for admission of a child for the diet; about the dietitian's role in teaching the parents before admission and during the admission; and in the next chapter we will talk about the most labor-intensive part of all—the fine-tuning of the diet. We have skipped over the single greatest impediment to implementation of the diet, the lack of adequately trained dietitians *who also have sufficient time* to implement the diet properly.

For example:

- If a hospital-based dietitian properly calculates the diet for a child and then sends that family home to calculate their own meal plans, the family is unlikely to be successful. The parent will quickly be overwhelmed.
- If the single dietitian for a large teaching hospital send a family home and then responds to their phone queries by saying, "I am hospital-based and do not handle out-patients," that child is unlikely to be successfully maintained on the diet.
- If there is one dietitian for a ketogenic diet program who is out on maternity leave for six months, what happens to the patients who have recently started on the diet? What happens to the program?

The dietitian's role is the weakest part of the way we have laid out our ketogenic diet program. This becomes apparent when others attempt to replicate our program. Our program started with a dedicated dietitian with years of experience, Mrs. Kelly. As our program grew, she retired from the hospital and was able to devote a large portion of her time to managing and fine-tuning the increasing numbers of patients that we are currently beginning on the diet each month. When we use the term *dietitian* in this book, we have been referring to the role that Mrs. Kelly has played in our program. Most hospitals, including Johns Hopkins, now have fewer dietitians than they had in the past, and those dietitians have more and different duties and are often unable to provide the amount of time required with these families. Additionally, much of what needs to be done with the parents occurs outside the hospital, both before admission and after discharge.

To run a successful ketogenic diet program, a person is needed to play those out-patient roles—as well as the in-hospital teaching.

- That person does not need to be a traditionally trained dietitian or nutritionist.
- That person must be someone who is trained in the calculation of the diet and experienced in the many pitfalls that parents experience as the diet is being initiated.
- That person must be someone who is patient, dedicated, with common sense, and experienced.

We call such an individual a "ketocoach."

A "ketocoach" should *only* work together with and under the supervision of the hospital-based ketogenic diet team.

In running our program, we have trained several nurses to be "ketocoaches." They have worked with Mrs. Kelly and are capable of fulfilling the role we have designated, "the dietitian's role." This includes everything from screening candidates for the diet to scheduling admissions, working with insurance programs, teaching in the hospital, calculating the diet, fine-tuning it after discharge, and counseling parents and children. We have managed to build their salaries into the hospital charge.

We have also selected some parents whose children have been on the diet and designated them as "parent advisors." We have tried to assign to each new family a parent who has successfully learned the diet for their own child, one whom the new parent can call for little tips. "Where can I find a sugar-free toothpaste?" "Jerry refuses to drink his cream. What can I do?" These are important details that physicians clearly do not know, which most dietitians do not have experience with or time for, but which parents who have already had their children on the diet have previously solved. Smoothing out these inevitable questions and bumps in the road to success often determine whether the diet will be a success or a failure. We would urge each ketogenic diet program to develop a group of "super moms" (or "super dads") as advisors who will supplement and become a part of the medical team. They will make life easier, and the program far more successful.

Several of our programs have used well-trained parent-advisors to supplement the dietitian/ketocoach member of the team.

These parent-advisors can be:

- a repository of practical information about the diet, from teaching other parents to read labels to locating specific foods;
- counselors to parents who think their child may be a candidate for the diet;
- a source of referral to centers where the diet is successfully implemented;
- a source of support during the fine-tuning of the diet.
- leaders of local support groups of parents whose children are on the diet.

Ketocoaches and parent-advisors should always work as a part of an established ketogenic diet program under medical supervision.

Reimbursement and rewarding of parent-advisors is a problem. Most of ours have been generous volunteers, but the task can be burdensome and time-consuming. They must be taught and encouraged to set limits. Parent-advisors must be trained to say "no" or "not now." They must be given the authority to say, "I think you have enough meal plans" or "Use your own judgment." When asked to play larger roles in a specific program, the program should seek to provide some reimbursement for both out-of-pocket expenses, such as telephone and postage, and for the time spent. If the parent-advisor is asked to volunteer for a limited time each day, week, or month, or to support a few families during their initial months on the diet, the job can be rewarding for both the advisor and the program.

Fine-Tuning the Diet

During the first few weeks that a child is on the ketogenic diet, lines of communication should be kept wide open among parents, doctors, and the supervising dietitian. It is only natural that a period of fine-tuning may be needed as the family becomes accustomed to preparing the diet and integrating it into their life, and as the unique complex machine that is every child's body becomes adjusted to its new fuel.

The most important thing for a parent to remember during this period is: you can persevere! If your child is doing well on the diet, terrific! But if there is a problem, you can solve it through open communication and thoughtful effort from all members of the team. If seizures are controlled for even a few days at the start, the diet is likely to work; breakthrough seizures imply not that the diet has failed, but that more fine-tuning is needed. If seizures are improved, less frequent, or less severe, further improvement is likely as the diet is adjusted.

Calorie allotments, the ratio of fats to protein and carbohydrate, meal plans, liquid intake, and anticonvulsant medications are some of the factors that may have to be adjusted during the fine-tuning period. The physician will be on the lookout for medical difficulties, and the dietitian will be ready to help plan new menus for a child who wants strawberry ice cream for breakfast or strongly desires ketchup on a steak.

Some children start the diet and need no help until it is time to shift to a lower ketogenic ratio and start phasing off it one to two years later, but for those whose diet requires fine-tuning the most important thing to remember is: tackle that problem! Identify the problem, communicate openly, and the solution will probably come.

I got a call from the father of a two-year-old who had just gone home from the hospital where the diet had been initiated. The mom had spent the five days in the hospital sleeping by the child's bed and was consequently exhausted. The child didn't seem to want to eat the meals the mom had prepared, and the father reported that the child was weak, sleepy, and irritable.

"We can't live like this!" he told me over the phone.

"How many seizures was she having last week, before she went into the hospital?" I asked.

"More than a hundred every day."

"How many did she have during the starvation?"

"About ten a day."

"How many did she have yesterday at home?"

"One!"

"I think that we should not give up the diet so fast. Let's look at why she might be so sleepy and irritable," I said. It turned out that she had developed a fever, and her pediatrician found a urinary tract infection, which was treated. Now she is doing just fine.

—JF

BE A SLEUTH

Q: If a child had no seizures while fasting but has a seizure upon arrival home from the hospital, what should the parents do?

A: (a) Panic.
    (b) Abandon the diet.
    (c) Try to trace the cause.
    (d) Blame the doctor.

The correct answer, as you may have guessed, is (c) Try to trace the cause. If a child is having problems on the diet, the parents and the rest of the diet team must become private eyes. It often takes a detective's spirit to locate the source of a problem and fix it.

The most common cause of a problem with the diet is that the child is getting the wrong amount or the wrong balance of food and liquid.

There could be many reasons why the amount or balance of food and liquid are off:

- Is there an opportunity for the child to eat extra food at school or while playing at a friend's house?
- Is the diet prescription correctly calculated? Are commercial foods being used?
- If commercial foods are used, are they the exact brands and items called for in the menu?
- Check the label—has the manufacturer changed ingredients?
- If calculations were made by computer, are the database entries for the ingredients correct?
- Everything should be measured on a gram scale except free fluids.
- Are Group B vegetables being measured properly, differently from Group A vegetables?
- Are vegetables being weighed cooked or raw as specified?
- Are the peaches packed in water, as they should be, rather than in glucose-containing syrup or fruit juice?
- Is there a soft-hearted grandparent in the picture who is encouraging the child to cheat "just a little"?

We cannot list every possible problem and solution in this book, but the principle to remember is: be a sleuth. Think it through. Don't give up. Look for clues. Has there been unusual weight gain? Weight loss? A sudden bout of seizures? A change in the number or kind of seizures at a certain time of the day or week? Problems following a certain meal plan? An illness?

If a problem develops, the parents should examine every aspect of their child's food and liquid intake, play habits, pharmaceuticals, and time with babysitters and grandparents. The dietitian should listen to a parent describing exactly how each meal is prepared. If the dietitian cannot solve the problem, the physician may need to get involved. With persistence you can most likely isolate the problem and correct it.

Jessica came in for a checkup after a year on the diet and she was doing great. She talked like a little adult whereas before the diet she had difficulty making sentences at all because her mind was so full of seizures. She was still having some seizures, though. What she told us was that her grandmother liked to give her candy even though the candy gave her seizures.

She said she was going to change that, though. She was going to start saying, "I can't have any more candy, Grandma. I'm on a special diet and I have to stay on my diet because I don't like having seizures!" Jessica has had to stay on the diet for longer than the usual period of time. She would probably have gotten off sooner if her grandmother hadn't cheated.

—MK

REMEMBER!

Not every child becomes seizure-free. Not every child becomes medication-free. After working carefully with the keto team for a month or more, you will have to decide if there is enough improvement to continue.

THE MOST COMMON PROBLEMS

Some of the most common problems and difficulties that children experience while adjusting to the ketogenic diet are discussed here. For each of these problems we have suggested some solutions. Remember to have patience, and always keep in mind the goal of achieving as much seizure control as you can.

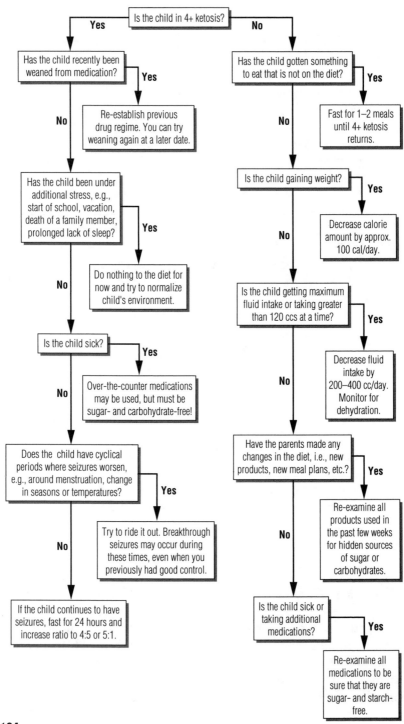

Is the child in 4+ ketosis?

Yes → Has the child recently been weaned from medication?
- **Yes** → Re-establish previous drug regime. You can try weaning again at a later date.
- **No** → Has the child been under additional stress, e.g., start of school, vacation, death of a family member, prolonged lack of sleep?
  - **Yes** → Do nothing to the diet for now and try to normalize child's environment.
  - **No** → Is the child sick?
    - **Yes** → Over-the-counter medications may be used, but must be sugar- and carbohydrate-free!
    - **No** → Does the child have cyclical periods where seizures worsen, e.g., around menstruation, change in seasons or temperatures?
      - **Yes** → Try to ride it out. Breakthrough seizures may occur during these times, even when you previously had good control.
      - **No** → If the child continues to have seizures, fast for 24 hours and increase ratio to 4:5 or 5:1.

No → Has the child gotten something to eat that is not on the diet?
- **Yes** → Fast for 1–2 meals until 4+ ketosis returns.
- **No** → Is the child gaining weight?
  - **Yes** → Decrease calorie amount by approx. 100 cal/day.
  - **No** → Is the child getting maximum fluid intake or taking greater than 120 ccs at a time?
    - **Yes** → Decrease fluid intake by 200–400 cc/day. Monitor for dehydration.
    - **No** → Have the parents made any changes in the diet, i.e., new products, new meal plans, etc.?
      - **Yes** → Re-examine all products used in the past few weeks for hidden sources of sugar or carbohydrates.
      - **No** → Is the child sick or taking additional medications?
        - **Yes** → Re-examine all medications to be sure that they are sugar- and starch-free.

HUNGER

The ketogenic diet will initially be calculated to provide approximately 75 percent of the calories normally recommended for a child's age and ideal weight. This should be enough to sustain most children without weight loss. They should remain close to the ideal weight for their age and height and should gain little or no weight for at least the first year while on the diet.

As the physical quantity of food is smaller than normal, many children are going to feel hungry during the first week or two of the diet. Overweight children will have their diets calculated to include some weight loss, which may cause feelings of hunger early in the diet. On the other hand, ketosis itself decreases the appetite. So try to determine whether a child is really hungry or just trying to manipulate the parents. Or it might be that the parents feel pity for the child or guilt about the diet.

Most children are able to tolerate some feelings of hunger and will stop feeling hungry between meals as their stomach and appetite adjust to fit the food they are consuming. Unless the hunger is severe or the child absolutely refuses to cooperate, we recommend that parents deal with it without trying to add extra calories to the diet, at least for the first few weeks.

Tricks to modify hunger without increasing calories include:

- chewing on ice chips;
- drinking decaffeinated diet soda or seltzer instead of water for at least part of the liquid allotment;
- eating a leaf of lettuce twice a day with meals;
- eating Group A vegetables or 10 percent fruits, of which greater quantities are allowed;
- making sure that foods such as vegetables are patted dry so that water is not part of the weight;
- recalculating the plan into four equal meals, or three meals and a snack, while maintaining a constant level of calories and the proper ketogenic ratio.

FIGURE 7   KETOGENIC DIET DECISION TREE—to be used when a child with previous control begins having seizures.

● ●

WEIGHT GAIN/WEIGHT LOSS

It takes 3,500 calories to gain a pound. If a child has gained a pound in one month, then 3,500 too many calories have been consumed. Dividing the calories by the number of days (thirty-one in a typical month) reveals that the child has consumed an average of 113 extra calories each day. By recalculating the diet at 113 fewer calories, the dietitian can stop the weight gain. On the other hand, if a child has lost a pound in one month, the same calculation will reveal that 113 calories should be added to the daily diet. With these additional calories, the child should gain back the lost pound in a month. Once the child's proper weight is reached, the gain or loss will stop.

● ●

If a child is losing too much weight or becomes uncooperative because of hunger, the calorie level should be increased in increments of about 100 to 150 calories. Enough time should pass between increments so that an evaluation can be made as to whether the child's weight is stabilized, whether seizure activity has occurred or increased, and whether hunger is under control.

If it is determined that extra calories are needed, instead of recalculating all the meal plans, a snack calculated at the prescribed ketogenic ratio for a predetermined number of extra calories may be added to the diet. Adding a ketogenic eggnog snack to the child's daily meal plan may be a convenient alternative to recalculating all the meals in the short term while adjustments to the diet are being made, or 12 grams of macadamia nuts equal 100 calories (macadamia nuts are naturally in the 4:1 ratio).

If a child cannot maintain constant ketosis or seizures are not under good control, *excess calories are almost always the culprit,* even when weight gain is not yet apparent. When problem-solving the diet, adjust calories *before* changing ratios.

Remember to take into account the child's activity level. Inactive children or those limited by severe handicaps will naturally need fewer calories.

THIRST

Liquid levels in the ketogenic diet are usually set at around 60 cc. per kilogram of body weight or approximately one cc. per calorie on the diet.

One of the goals of the diet is to maintain the body in a state slightly more dehydrated than normal, which is why liquid intake is restricted. Liquid levels must strike a balance between being high enough for adequate body function without being so high that they adversely affect the diet. Too little liquid can result in kidney stones.

Some children on the ketogenic diet feel very thirsty. It seems to be important for many children to space the consumption of liquids evenly throughout the day and not to give a thirsty child a big drink all at once, as this can sometimes cause breakthrough seizure activity and can also leave the child more thirsty later on. Some parents give their children a regular dose of water or diet soda (with no caffeine) every one to two hours during the day. Other children seem to be able to drink larger amounts of liquid with no seizures.

In hot climates or during summer months, the cream in the diet need not be counted as part of the allotted liquid. In effect, this raises the liquid allowance by the quantity of the cream.

If the level of liquid has been set too low, thirst may persist and may be accompanied by symptoms of dehydration, such as dry lips and skin. Painful renal stones, hyperuricemia, and acidosis are also occasional by-products of too low liquid levels. These conditions can usually be cured rapidly in consultation with the dietitian or physician by raising liquid levels while monitoring ketones to ensure that ketosis is maintained. These conditions fortunately should not normally interfere with continuation of the diet. When it is necessary to adjust liquid levels, this should be done in increments of approximately 100–200 cc. per day.

SLEEPINESS

The most likely cause of sleepiness on the ketogenic diet is an elevated medication level. Medication levels frequently rise in the blood of children on the ketogenic diet even without a change in dosage, perhaps because there is less food in the stomach or because of the changes that occur in the brain's metabolism on the diet. Medication levels should thus be monitored carefully during the fasting and diet initiation period. Medications that cause drowsiness, such as phenobarbital, should be decreased if sleepiness occurs. Except during the first days, the diet itself should not cause sleepiness or a persistent decrease in energy levels.

Fatigue is *not* a side effect of the diet. Indeed, many children on the ketogenic diet become more alert and energetic than they were prior to the diet, partly as a result of taking fewer medications and partly as a result of having fewer seizures.

As mentioned in Chapter 5, hypoglycemia or low blood sugar levels can also cause drowsiness during the initial fasting period. With the possible exception of children under fourteen months of age, blood sugar levels should return to normal within a few days of starting the diet.

> When she came to us, Jennifer was tied in a wheelchair. She was so drugged she could not stand or even hold her head up. She was already on a low protein diet because her liver had been damaged by medication. Five days after she started the initial fast and ketogenic diet she was running down the hall! Everybody was so excited. Back home, she didn't need naps anymore. Her anticonvulsants were stopped. She was doing so well and not having any seizures. Then the seizures came back, a little bit at first, and of course we had to recheck everything. It turned out that Jennifer liked nuts. She was allowed two "free" nuts per day. But her mother had started giving her extra nuts, seven per day because she was begging for them and they made her so happy. When we went back to two nuts a day the seizures came back under control.
>
> —MK

FINE-TUNING MEAL PLANS

The meal plans themselves also may need fine-tuning. Physical reasons, such as weight loss or weight gain, may necessitate tuning the meal plans, or it may be a question of taste. After parents start on the diet, they will learn from their children what works and what does not work for them. The child who loves chocolate popsicles, for instance, may need to have chocolate popsicles calculated into every lunch and dinner. The child who develops an aversion to sauerkraut may need to have a hot dog meal reconfigured to include celery or applesauce instead.

Once parents get the hang of using their gram scales and making up menus, some want to add little treats to the diet to increase the child's enjoyment of meals or ability to participate in family events. Adding ingredients is limited by the mathematical confines of the ketogenic ratio, by the child's protein requirement, and by the dietitian's time to prepare and check calculations. Fats, carbohydrates, and protein must be kept in proper balance, of course, and enough protein must be supplied in the diet to support a child's physical development. Still, parents and dietitians can find ways to include treats for the children that are properly calculated into the diet.

Carbohydrates eaten in the form of Ritz Bits will take away from those available to be eaten as fruits or vegetables, but some parents think this is worth the pleasure that the treats give to their child during the limited time span of the diet. After all, the object of the ketogenic diet is to control seizures; within the limits of this goal, the diet should be made as easy as possible for the child to live with.

Parents should carefully research any and all new foods they wish to introduce into the diet, especially commercially processed foods. Foods whose protein, fat, and carbohydrate content are not clearly labeled should be avoided. So-called diet foods or sugar-free foods such as chewing gum may contain carbohydrates that make them inappropriate for the diet or at least require that they be calculated in. This topic is addressed more thoroughly in Chapters 4 and 7.

CONSTIPATION

Because of the small volume of food and high concentration of fat in this diet, constipation can become a problem. Constipation may cause stomach pains and discomfort. Fortunately, it does not have to be an obstacle to continuing the diet.

Using Group A vegetables in meal plans can help increase the bulk and fiber in the diet a little bit. Also, two leaves of lettuce, or about one-half cup of chopped lettuce, are allowed each day as so-called free food. Giving a child lettuce with lunch and dinner can also increase bulk and fiber.

Make sure that the child is receiving the proper amount of liquid. Increasing liquid levels by 100–150 cc. may help combat constipation.

If a child continues to have problems with constipation, laxatives or enemas may help. Full-strength enemas should not be used regularly, however, as they can affect the lining of the intestine. One mother found that a quarter dose of Baby Fleet enema, given every other day, helped her son to have regular bowel movements. Small amounts of Colace (1% solution or suppository) or Milk of Magnesia might also prove effective. Like other medications, laxatives must be sugar-free. MCT oil in small amounts can be calculated into the child's diet and helps with constipation. The oil will replace some of the fat requirement at each meal. Cal-Mag is also said to be useful. (See Appendix A.)

MEDICATION LEVELS

Reducing anticonvulsant medications is one of the primary goals of the ketogenic diet. Many children on the diet are able to stop taking all anticonvulsant medications and never have to go on them again. The situation varies for each individual.

As described previously, blood levels of medications tend to rise in children as they start the diet, even with no increase in dosage. Binding of medications to proteins may also change with the body's acidosis. Thus, levels should be watched carefully, especially in the initiation stage of the diet. As a rule of thumb, phenobarbital is usually dropped or markedly decreased at the onset of fasting. Depending on what medications the child is taking, one other medication may also be decreased or stopped at this time. If the child is doing well at home and not having seizures, the other medications are gradually tapered off. Diamox® should also be discontinued before starting the diet because it also acts to increase acidosis.

Don't be in too much of a hurry. Get the diet working first. When the family and child are on a stable routine, one medicine at a time can be gradually reduced and eliminated. If medication is reduced in this systematic, gradual fashion and the child has a few seizures, it becomes easy to figure out the reason.

The key to weaning children off their anticonvulsant medications during the fine-tuning period is to separate the effects of decreasing dosages of medications from other factors in the diet. In other words, don't reduce medications at the same time as adjusting the food. If a child has breakthrough seizures while the medicine is being reduced, don't assume that the seizures are a result of the tapering off. Look for all the possible factors and try to determine whether or not the reduction in medication is the cause.

BREAKTHROUGH SEIZURE ACTIVITY

As mentioned previously, the most common cause of seizure activity in a child who is achieving good results on the ketogenic diet is that the child is getting the wrong amount or the wrong balance of food and liquid.

Possible causes to look for include:

- The child is being given food that is not on the diet.
- The child is eating extra food in secret.
- The child has gained weight—excess calories!
- Liquid is not being spaced out enough.
- Food is being prepared incorrectly.
- Information on food ingredients is incorrect.
- The diet has been miscalculated.
- The child is sick.
- The child has come out of ketosis for some other reason.

The level of urinary ketosis may vary with the time of day. It is usually lower in the morning and higher later in the day. This may be a function of bladder activity, of how much urine is being produced in relation to the ketones. This natural variation in the level of ketones as measured in the urine does not necessarily indicate a problem if it is not accompanied by seizures.

If seizures do occur, parents, doctors, and dietitians should think about the elements of the diet and try to isolate possible causes for the breakthrough activity.

The first thing to look for is whether the child has had an opportunity to eat something that is not on the diet. Food may have been given by someone or taken by the child. One child was found to be sneaking sugared toothpaste in an upstairs bathroom. One was slipping out of bed at night and raiding the refrigerator. Another girl had a seizure on Sunday, and her mother found to her dismay that she had been given a lollipop by a well-meaning grownup at church.

Another possible cause of breakthrough activity on the diet is a calorie level that is set too high. If the body takes in more calories than are needed for maintenance, it will store fat from those extra calories so that less fat is available for burning and fewer ketones are generated. As few as 100 calories too many per day can upset ketosis. At an excess of 100 calories/day, it takes an entire month before any weight gain is seen. Therefore, some caloric adjustments can be made based on low ketone levels.

Weight gain on the diet is an indication that calorie levels are set too high. A child should rarely gain more than one to two pounds during the entire first year on the diet. If good seizure control was obtained during fasting but seizures returned on the diet, something is wrong with the way the diet was calculated! It may be too many calories, too much carbohydrate, or a miscalculation. Sometimes better control may be achieved by using a 4.5:1 ratio or even a 5:1 ratio for a period of time. The higher the diet ratio, the more restricted food options get, so the implications of raising the diet ratio should be considered before it is prescribed.

Infants under one year of age often have difficulty maintaining ketosis and normal blood sugar levels on the diet. We do not recommend even trying it on an infant under one year of age.

Last but not least, sickness and fever can cause seizure activity to occur. An isolated seizure during illness requires no action on the part of the parents.

• •

The diet is highly successful for most children with difficult seizures. But it does not control everyone's seizures.

• •

THERE MAY NOT BE A 100 PERCENT SOLUTION

In studies to date, one-third of all children who stick with the diet stop having seizures and many do not need medication any longer. An additional 25–30 percent, while not completely seizure-free, are improved enough that the parents choose to continue the diet for at least one year. This improvement may involve a decrease in seizures and/or the better behavior and intelligence that comes with ketosis and decreased medications.

Some children continue to have seizure activity even if the diet is perfectly calibrated.

A reasonable aim for parents as their child starts on the ketogenic diet is to achieve as much seizure control as possible with as few medications as possible. Improvements in behavior, mood, mental alertness, and a general sense of well-being are additional benefits that the diet often brings. If parents set a goal of total seizure control, they may be setting themselves up for disappointment. Total control may not be possible.

After trying the diet for the initial one-month period, and after working with the dietitian and physician to figure out if greater control can be achieved by adjusting food or medications, parents of children who have not responded to the diet or who have improved only moderately have to make a decision. These parents must weigh the benefits of the diet for their child against its burdens. Then they have to decide whether or not it is worthwhile for them to continue on the diet.

DON'T BE DAUNTED

If there are indications that a child is being helped by the diet but some problems remain, get into a fine-tuning mode. Be a sleuth. Parents, physicians, and dietitians must work together. Figure out the possible causes of the problems and root them out. Only then can you say that you have done everything you can to help a child reap the benefits of the ketogenic diet.

SEVEN

Making It Work at Home and on the Road

Be creative, but follow the rules exactly. Follow the rules exactly, but be creative. Remember these two principles and you can successfully integrate the ketogenic diet into your family life. As long as you follow the rules, you and your child can do just about anything you ever did before the diet started.

TIME-SAVERS

Most families find that the diet is very time-consuming to plan and prepare at first, but it gets faster and easier as they become accustomed to using the gram scale and planning meals in advance.

Much time can be saved by preparing and storing meals or parts of meals in advance. You can refrigerate many foods for a few days or freeze them for a week or more. Following are some time-saving tips from parents who have experienced the diet:

- I cut up his favorite vegetables and keep them in plastic bags in the refrigerator for a few days. Then I can take them out and weigh a meal in no time.

- I usually make cream popsicles once a week. He has one after every dinner.
- We measure a day or two of meals at a time and put them in containers. That way we only have to do the weighing about every other day. Also, we can either serve the meals at home or take them with us if we are eating out.
- Whenever someone is celebrating a birthday at school, I know what to make for him—I send him in with a fruit-topped ketogenic cheesecake so he can have something good to eat, too.
- I put a cream shake in a container and freeze it so he can eat it later as ice cream, or let it thaw back down to a shake.
- I always keep some tuna or chicken salad and bags of cut-up vegetables stored in the refrigerator in case I can't be there to fix dinner myself. He also takes these stored meals to school. Salads are our savior.

GOING TO SCHOOL AND ON OTHER SHORT TRIPS

Anything the family did before, they can still do on the diet—it will just take a little more planning. Every parent who has been through the diet has tips to offer:

- The key to making the diet "portable" is reusable storage containers.
- Cold food is easier to transport than hot food.
- It is easy to get food microwaved in a restaurant.
- It is usually easier to weigh and assemble a whole meal or several meals at home in advance than to weigh food on the road.

Eggnog is the traditional replacement meal, designed for all-purpose substitution in case of travel, sickness, or emergencies that make it difficult to prepare a meal. Eggnog is a complete meal-in-one (except for vitamin supplements), which is part of what makes it so convenient. It can be made up in every ketogenic ratio (see Chapter 4). Most children like the taste. Also, each sip is ketogenically balanced, so they don't have to drink all of it, or drink it all at once, to get its ketogenic effect. Eggnog should not be used too often in place of meals because it does not have the nutritional value of fruits and vegetables, but it can be extremely useful in a pinch.

We carried a small cooler with an ice pack in it everywhere. In the morning, we fixed the whole day's meal before going out. It got so that even if we weren't going anywhere we would set up all the meals for the day and stick them in Tupperware containers in the refrigerator. If we were going on a long trip, we would take about two days' worth of food with us in the cooler and bring our scale. Also, we always carried extra ingredients that we knew might be hard to buy, like cocoa. Everyone has a microwave, even on airplanes. We could give a fancy restaurant a couple of Tupperware containers and instructions for how long to cook things, and they would bring the food out on their own plate. Everybody was really cooperative.

—RZ

Following are some meal ideas for taking to school or on short outings. Each meal requires several reusable containers for storage.

- Tuna, chicken, or egg salad with mayonnaise
  Fresh vegetables (cucumber, carrot, cherry tomato, celery)
  Sugar-free Jell-O with whipped cream sweetened with Sucaryl

- Celery or cucumber boats stuffed with tuna salad, cream cheese and butter, or peanut butter and butter
  Chocolate milkshake, whipped and frozen overnight

- Sandwich rolled in lettuce (chicken, cheese, turkey, or roast beef with mayonnaise)
  Water-packed canned peaches
  Chocolate milk (cream diluted with water and flavored with baking chocolate or pure chocolate extract and saccharin)

- Cottage cheese with chopped fruit or vegetables and mayonnaise
  Vanilla milkshake, whipped and frozen overnight

- Fruit-topped cheesecake, frozen overnight: a one-dish meal

Foods frozen overnight and taken out in the morning soften to a pudding-like consistency by lunch time. Foods to be taken to school or on short outings can be wrapped in foil or carried in a thermal pouch or cooler for extra insulation, to help stay either warm or cold. Whipped cream can be stored for a few hours and still keep its body.

> When we went to Disneyland we just took a big cooler with three whole days of meals in labeled containers. Once we let him get a hot dog from the stand so he could feel like he was having a special treat. I wouldn't say it was easy doing all that planning, but for us it wasn't too difficult.
>
> —RZ

If you are going out to eat at a restaurant and you want your child to have a hot meal, call first to make sure the restaurant has a microwave that can be used for heating your food. If you are giving the child a cold meal, ask the restaurant to bring an extra plate, which will make the food look nice and add to the feeling of family togetherness.

Parents approach the diet in various ways. One mother kept her child out of school for a year and hired an in-home teacher because she did not want him to be tempted by seeing other children eat (we do not advise this). Another was persuaded by the child himself that going out was a good thing: the pleasure for the whole family of being at a restaurant was greater than the annoyance of having to bring the child's food along or the pain of his seeing other people eating food he could not have. "It turned out I was much more afraid of temptation than he was," said the mother.

Another family went out as often as they had before the diet, routinely asking fancy restaurants to take prepared food in Tupperware containers, warm it in a microwave, and bring it back on the restaurant's china. "Restaurants were always happy to accommodate us," the father said.

BABYSITTERS AND OTHER MOM-LESS MEALS

In most households, the person who usually prepares the meals is occasionally unavailable—working late, sick, at a party, or otherwise engaged. Not to worry! With a little planning, someone else can easily put a meal together from your prepared ingredients.

Many parents store measured ingredients or prepared food a couple of days ahead of time in the refrigerator even when they are planning to be present to prepare each meal. The habit of preparing meals in advance both saves time on a routine basis and makes it easier to cope with special situations.

Some items can be measured and stored or frozen up to a week in advance:

Popsicles	Meat
Cream shakes	Chicken
Cheesecake	Eggnog
Ice cream	Spaghetti squash
Sugar-free Jell-O	

Note that foods such as ice cream must be calculated and carefully labeled to go with a particular meal that you plan to make. This is because different meal plans use varying amounts of cream, and ingredients such as fruit or oil may need to be frozen into the ice cream, depending on what else is being served for supper. Other foods can be prepared, weighed, and stored in the refrigerator one or two days in advance:

Cooked meat or chicken portions	D-Zerta gelatin
Tuna, egg, or chicken salads	Vegetables
Cream portions for whipping	Fresh fruit
Tomato sauce	
Sliced or grated cheese	

If a parent leaves measured ingredients and instructions, a sibling or babysitter can easily carry out final assembly of the meal. Make these meals simple: try to think of meals that can be put in one microwave dish and cooked or reheated (stew, squash/cheese/butter casserole) or meals that do not need cooking at all (tuna salad).

LONG TRIPS

Yes, the family can take vacations. Longer trips by necessity involve more planning than shorter ones. Many families who take long vacations choose to stay in places where they can cook, such as friends' condominiums or motels with kitchenettes, rather than in hotels. They sometimes take eggnog for the road instead of a solid meal. They take their scales, and call ahead to make sure that places where they will be staying have heavy cream and microwaves available. They take coolers full of prepared ingredients for the first couple of days, and hard-to-find staples such as artificial sweetener and baking chocolate. If they are staying in a hotel with no kitchen, they might take a camping stove to cook on. They take a lot of storage containers.

They take their calcium and multivitamin supplements, too, of course, because they never forget those.

Apart from the nuisance of planning, the diet should be no obstacle to family fun. There is no reason why a child should not live a rich, full, and healthy life while on the ketogenic diet.

He skied this year for the first time in ages. He skied like you wouldn't believe. He's swimming, he's playing ball. He's definitely had a happier life on the diet.

—CC

BE CREATIVE

Being creative can mean compensating for a small quantity of cucumbers and carrots by slicing them in tall, thin strips and fanning them out to cover more plate space. It can mean dressing up the cream as a toasted almond ice cream, whipped into a mound flavored with almond extract and sweetener and sprinkled with a crushed almond. Let the child sprinkle on the nuts for fun.

There are lots of calorie-free ways to keep the food lively. Play with variables that add interest, not calories:

- shapes;
- natural food colors or food coloring;
- herbs and spices;
- pure flavoring extracts;
- pretending.

> We freeze his diet decaffeinated pop in miniature ice cube trays. These make refreshing little treats. He has a small amount as a goodie before bed. We give it to him in a wine glass to make it fancy and special.
>
> We also make popsicles out of his pop. If it's clear pop, we let him mix in food coloring drops, so he is not only involved but also learning. This adds lots of laughs when his teeth and lips turn green or blue or purple!
>
> —EH

Peaches can be swapped for strawberries, carrots for beets, beef for chicken. Combine fruits or vegetables for variety—peaches with a couple of raspberries on top, or asparagus with carrots. Switching the foods around helps give variety to the meals. This not only keeps a child interested, but also tends to lead to better nutrition.

The pieces of the diet are like Lego parts: you cannot bend them individually, but you can build them into a hundred different shapes.

Of course, some kids prefer to eat the same thing over and over again. Some parents end up making only six out of their thirty meal plans because that's all their child likes to eat. If a child asks for the same meal again and again, there is nothing wrong with that. But if a child wants variety, there's plenty of room for creativity within the diet.

He has his special "pizza." It's just cheese on a slice of tomato, cut into triangles the shape of pizza slices. But he loves it. It's pizza to him!

—EH

Follow the Rules Exactly

If the rules are followed exactly, the family will know the child was given the best possible chance to obtain the maximum benefits of the diet. The effect of the ketogenic diet is directly related to the food that is eaten and the liquid that is drunk. This may seem obvious, but it is the factor that makes the diet work.

Especially when using commercial products, knowing the precise content of the food is essential. Buy the exact brand specified by the dietitian. The same product, such as bologna, made by different manufacturers may have very different proportions of protein, fat, and carbohydrates. The dietitian will have based diet calculations on the proportions of a given brand, so if a new brand is used the calculations may have to be changed.

About a week after he started the diet, my son was doing great. Then we went to the store and bought some commercial turkey loaf. The meal plan called for turkey, so we thought turkey loaf would be just as good. Well, I don't know what was in it, but my son had a very bad day the next day. That's when we discovered that when the meal plan says turkey, it means plain, fresh turkey, not turkey loaf. You have to follow instructions to the letter.

—FD

It would never have occurred to us to eat something that wasn't allowed on the diet. Even when we were allowed to, when the diet was ending, we had a hard time imagining eating food that hadn't been allowed before.

—CC

If a different brand needs to be introduced, the parents or dietitian must research the product carefully, even if it means calling the manufacturer to find out. Make sure that the new brand is properly calculated into the meal plans.

Even when a commercial product is known and used regularly, formulations and commercial recipes can change. If breakthrough seizures develop, this should be one source of suspicion. At the risk of repeating ourselves, ingredients of commercially prepared foods, which are beyond your power to control, have to be watched very carefully. Be cautious in reading labels as well. By law, products that contain less than 1 gram of an ingredient per serving may be listed as zero, so a product that you thought had no carbohydrates may actually have up to .9 grams. If used on a regular basis, this can add up to a lot of excess carbohydrates.

There was one time we wanted to try a new brand of sausage. We read the label very carefully and checked it with Mrs. Kelly and everything. But shortly after we started including it in her diet, our daughter began feeling very shaky, what she described as "wobbly" inside. Dr. Freeman said it sounded like she might be trying to break through with seizures. We're pretty sure it was because of that sausage; either the label was wrong or it referred to raw quantities and we were using cooked, or something. We went back to the old brand, and then she was fine.

—MH

With basic ingredients such as fresh meat, fruit, and vegetables, this is not as much of a problem, although the exact content of even fresh produce does vary slightly from one source to another.

If your child is having problems with the diet, always consider the food—both its quantity and content—as the most likely culprit.

Are there commercial products in the diet? Has the source of cream or bacon changed? Is the cream still 36 to 40 percent fat? Different children have different amounts of tolerance for variations in food content. It is the little things that often spell the difference between success and failure of the diet. If your child is doing well on the diet, then obviously you shouldn't worry. You should simply continue to be careful.

GET THE WHOLE FAMILY INVOLVED

You and your child are making a tremendous effort to stick to the diet in pursuit of a tremendous goal, and you need everyone's cooperation and encouragement. You can weigh the food in advance, but if you are not there at dinner time, someone else—an older sister or brother, a grandmother—can put it in the microwave and serve it. A child on the diet and all the child's sisters and brothers, relatives, friends, and teachers should understand that even tiny amounts of cheating can spoil the overall effect of the diet, and that their friendship, support, and encouragement are crucial to its success.

> Everything went really well for us. We were really careful, read every label, never gave her anything that wasn't allowed. We followed the rules to the nth degree. And she never had any more seizures.
>
> —MH

EIGHT

Going Off the Diet

The ketogenic diet is not forever! When the time comes, it should be stopped gradually over a period of approximately one year. Children traditionally remain on the 4:1 diet ratio for two years, or until they have been seizure-free without medication for one full year. Then they switch to a 3:1 diet ratio for six months. If they remain seizure-free, this is followed by a 2:1 ratio for six months, after which they are weaned off the diet and can eat any foods they want.

This traditional regimen for easing off the diet may be more cautious than is absolutely necessary, but we believe it is better to err on the side of caution. Withdrawing too abruptly from the diet could bring back seizures, and possibly even status epilepticus, wiping out all those months of discipline. The length of time a child has to stay on the 4:1 ratio is sometimes extended by a year or two if a child has not stuck to the reg-

> Toward the end we started letting him smell things. The other kids would give him a sniff of what they were eating, and he would say, "I can have that when I'm off the diet, right?"
>
> —CC

She was a junior bridesmaid at a wedding the day she went off the diet. That was when she was twelve. We had checked with Mrs. Kelly and agreed to let her eat cake at the reception. All of us were very apprehensive. There had been a lot of anxiety each time we cut the ratio, but she kept doing well, so sweets were the last test. Nobody else at the reception really knew what we were going through—it was a private thing among us and our very close friends. When she ate the cake and had no problems, it was thrilling for us. After that we were probably cautious for another week or two. Now she won't look at whipped cream, but she eats just like a typical teenager—pizza and candy and all the typical teenage food.

—MH

imen strictly, or if there is some other reason to think more time on the diet will help the child to a greater degree.

For some children whose seizures have not been completely controlled, it is possible to continue the diet beyond two years to maintain the degree of control that has been achieved. Continuing the diet in this

We had been down to a 1:1 ratio for a few months when one day [the doctor] said, "Why don't you take him out for an ice cream sundae—you're off the diet!" Well, I couldn't quite do that but we did take him for a steak and potato dinner. Then about an hour later I got him a little dish of mint chocolate chip ice cream. It was very dramatic for me to see him eat a real meal. And for him, too—his little eyes were watering. It was a tear-jerking experience. We had finally made it!

He used to be an extremely picky eater but now he just really enjoys eating.

—JS

case is an alternative to the increased medications that will probably be needed when the diet is stopped. If a child who has been well-controlled on the diet begins to have seizures again once it has ended (this is very rare), it is possible to restart the diet.

There does not seem to be any chemical or metabolic reason for stopping the diet sooner rather than later; it is just good to get back to a normal life.

> After he had done perfectly for a year and a half on the 4:1 diet, we had done six months on the 3:1, and then a couple of months on the 2:1, when his sixth birthday was coming up. We asked him what he wanted, and he said pizza. Well, you're nervous as can be, but he was doing so well that we decided to stop the diet on his birthday, before the full six months of the 2:1 were up. We invited all the neighborhood kids in, and I put candles in the pizza. After he took the first bite, he looked up at me and said, "Dad, this is the best birthday present I've ever had."
>
> —RZ

On the other hand, some children who have responded exceptionally well to the diet start to come off it before the two-year mark is reached. This decision is often suggested by the parents and agreed to in consultation with the physicians.

ANXIETY AND RELIEF

It is natural for a parent to feel anxious when a child is going off the diet. After all that time spent planning and measuring food to an accuracy of a gram, it's hard to kick the habit! All we can tell nervous parents is that in ending the diet they should go as slowly as they want. And that once the diet is over, we're pretty sure they won't miss it.

After we had been on the 2:1 diet for about six weeks I asked what was next, and Mrs. Kelly said I could give him some popcorn with lots of butter. I was so nervous I was shaking when I gave it to him. He felt the same way. "Are you sure she said I could have popcorn?" he asked me.

I almost didn't know how to gradually withdraw the diet. When it came time to go off it, the thought of giving him a glass of low-fat milk instead of cream made me crazy with nerves.

—CC

A child can start going off the diet once the full benefits of the diet have been realized. Exactly when this invisible finish line has been crossed will vary for each child. But by the time a child has been on the diet rigidly for two years and is seizure-free, its long-term benefits will most likely have already been gained. If the EEG has returned to normal, for instance, it is likely to stay normal. Even if the EEG is still abnormal, it may be possible for the child who has been seizure-free for two years to go off the diet gradually without the return of seizures. The child is likely to remain seizure-free when normal eating is resumed if there have been no seizures with no medication during the diet.

Going off the diet was very liberating. At last we could go places without planning and thinking about every meal. We could spend a day at the mall. She could go to parties and eat what the other kids were having. It was great.

—MH

Lower ketogenic ratios are increasingly similar to regular meals. A 2:1 ratio will seem almost like a normal diet compared with the 4:1. There will be room for a lot more meat and vegetables, and even the possibility of some carbohydrates, which is why carbohydrates such as corn are included in the food database in the back of this book and in the accompanying computer database.

Once a child has been weaned down to a 2:1 ratio and has been on that ratio for a few months, we recommend that formerly forbidden foods be gradually introduced into the diet. We encourage parents to start with somewhat fatty foods, such as buttery popcorn, greasy French fries, and hamburgers. Sometimes we go to a 1:1 ratio for a few months, which can be useful as a tapering method even though at this ratio the child is no longer in ketosis. In general, though, when the gradually introduced foods have reached a point where the child is no longer in ketosis, you're home free!

> For me the diet really wasn't all that hard. There wasn't a single day when I resented having to weigh the meals. For me it was a very pleasant experience. It was just a miracle.
>
> —JS

Calculations

Section III

NINE

Calculating the Ketogenic Diet

INTRODUCTION

Calculating the ketogenic diet is three parts science and one part art. The art part is a combination of common sense, empathy, and intuition. In each case, a child's individual needs must be taken into account. The diet is generally based on 75 percent of the Recommended Daily Allowance (RDA) of calories for a child's ideal weight and height, but it can be modified for such factors as the child's activity level, natural rate of metabolism, and the climate of his or her hometown.

There are currently two different ways of calculating the ketogenic diet. The traditional method is by hand, using exchange lists and rounded nutritional values for simplicity. This method is cumbersome, time-consuming, and based to a certain extent on nutritional averages. It is, however, the tried-and-true method. More recently, a computer program that greatly simplifies calculation of the diet has been developed. The program may be purchased by calling the Epilepsy Association of Maryland at (410) 828-7700. The program can easily juggle the nutritional composition of several ingredients in a meal. It is more precise and uses newer, detailed data about the precise nutritional content of foods. It may result in slightly different numbers of calories and grams than the hand-calculation method.

One advantage of the hand-calculation method is the convenience of using exchange lists. It is easy for parents to switch from one Group A vegetable to another or one 10 percent fruit to another, depending on their child's whims or what is available in the grocery store. The precision of the computer calculations shows the minor differences between the content of, say, broccoli and carrots. We do not believe that these minor differences are of any importance. Therefore, once a meal plan has been calculated by computer, exchanges may still be made among the foods on the traditional exchange lists.

There are four main areas to which the physician's and dietitian's judgment must be applied in determining the input values for the ketogenic diet calculation:

- ideal weight;
- calories per kilogram;
- ketogenic ratio (fat to protein + carbohydrate);
- liquid allotment.

Ideal weight is based on a child's current height and weight, the size of the child's frame, a history of whether the child has recently gained or lost weight, and a comparison with the recommended weight shown in standard weight tables. The calories per kilogram level is based on a child's age, as discussed in more detail below. Calories per kilogram is fairly straightforward, although kids at borderline ages require a measure of judgment. Ideal weight and the calories per kilogram level are two sides of the same coin; when multiplied, they produce a child's total allotment of calories per day.

The initial ketogenic ratio is usually 4:1 unless a child is very young or very fat. We have found that very young children (under fifteen months) do better on a ratio of 3:1 or 3.5:1. A 3:1 ratio allows more protein (about 1.5 grams per kilogram of body weight vs. 1 gram per kilogram on a 4:1 ratio) than a higher ratio would, and more carbohydrates. Both promote health and body maintenance and help prevent the development of low blood sugar in infants. In the case of a very fat child, the 3:1 diet will be based on an ideal weight lower than the current weight, and this should lead to some weight loss.

In the case of the child who is severely underweight, you may want to base the child's calories/kg on the *current* weight. A child cannot both gain weight and maintain ketosis at the same time. By using the *current* weight, you can achieve ketosis and control seizures first and then *slowly* increase the calories by increments of 100 calories per day. If the child's weight is so low that it creates a medical problem, it should be corrected before starting the diet.

Although fluid restriction has not been well studied and its importance to the diet is not entirely clear, anecdotal evidence indicates that fluid intake levels may affect seizure control in children on the ketogenic diet. We generally set liquid allotments at 60–70 cc., or an average of 65 cc., per kilo of body weight per day, not to exceed two liters per day. Another way of figuring liquid is that the number of cubic centimeters of liquid should not exceed the number of calories on the diet. In summer or in hot climates, the cream in the diet is excluded from the liquid allotment.

As they are the most subjective areas of the diet, the categories discussed here should be among the first to be reexamined if problems arise or if seizure control is lacking when parents are doing everything right.

> The goal is to get good seizure control, and sometimes you have to be very strict to do that. People often don't mind being strict, though, if it works.
>
> —MK

THE CASES OF BRIAN AND ADAM

The thought process that goes into a typical ketogenic diet prescription can be illustrated by the example of Brian and Adam.

Brian is six years and two months old, small, and skinny for his age. He is 117.5 cm. tall (at fiftieth percentile) and weighs only eighteen kilos (forty pounds, at tenth percentile). Ideal weight for a child Brian's height, at fiftieth percentile, would be twenty-one kilos. His mother says he has lost almost seven pounds in the past few months because his latest medication was making him sick and he could not keep his food down.

Adam is a strapping, active four-year-old, short for his age and plump—he is 101 cm. and already weighs eighteen kilos (forty pounds, at seventy-fifth percentile). How should we set up the ketogenic diet calculation for Brian and Adam?

Although both boys actually weigh eighteen kilos, we would base their diet calculations on different ideal weights. We would like Brian to be closer to his ideal weight of twenty-one kilos, so in setting up the diet calculation we would use twenty-one kilos as his weight. This was about what he weighed a few months ago before he started losing weight, according to his mother, and it is what we think he should ideally weigh. He will probably be stronger at the higher weight if he can tolerate the extra calories while achieving seizure control.

On the other hand, we would base Adam's diet on a weight of sixteen kilos, which is the ideal, fiftieth-percentile weight for a child of Adam's age and height. We usually give fewer calories to overweight children than their current weights would dictate, as we find that this leads to better results.

We might allot slightly more liquid per kilo to Adam than to Brian, as Adam is a more active child. We would most likely start both boys on a 4:1 ratio, although if Adam were really fat, we might consider starting him on a 3:1 diet based on his ideal weight. As he moved from his current weight to his ideal weight, he would be burning his own body fat to supplement the diet.

If Brian's seizures are not well controlled on the 4:1 diet, investigate the extra calories as a potential culprit. If Adam, after an adjustment period, is so hungry that he becomes noncompliant or weak, or his lips are dry from thirst, his calorie and liquid levels may need adjusting, as discussed in Chapter 6. Thus the rules and calculation formula are only a starting point, not set in stone. Later we can fine-tune if necessary.

Once judgments are made about ideal weight, ketogenic ratio, and liquid allotment, the ketogenic diet can be calculated either by computer or by following the steps below. Although the computer software makes calculating the diet much faster and easier, it is useful to understand the steps of the calculation so that it can be modified if necessary to meet each child's individual needs.

GENERAL RULES FOR THE INITIAL KETOGENIC DIET CALCULATION

1. Calorie intake should be approximately 75 percent of the recommended calorie level for a child's age and ideal weight. The level may be higher for an especially active child. Calorie levels are listed in the "Calculating the Diet" section.

2. Ideal weight should be based on recognized standards, while factoring in individual circumstances such as recent weight loss or gain and the size of a child's frame.
3. Most children are started on a 4:1 ketogenic ratio. Very young (under fifteen months) or very fat children may be started on a 3:1 or 3.5:1 ratio of fat:protein + carbohydrates. Older adolescents can also be started on the 3:1 ratio to provide greater variety and quantities of food. If ketosis cannot be maintained, they can later be switched to a 3:5 or 4:1 ratio.
4. Liquid levels should be approximately 65 cc. per kilogram per day, with a little more liquid given to especially active children or children who live in hot climates, and a little less given to children who get very little exercise. As a rule of thumb, a child should not drink more cubic centimeters of liquid per day than the number of calories in his diet.
5. The diet must include a minimum of one gram of protein per kilogram of body weight per day to fulfill the body's needs for tissue repair, defense mechanisms, and growth. More protein may be included on 3:1 and 2:1 diets.
6. The ketogenic diet must be supplemented daily with calcium and a sugar-free, lactose-free multivitamin. Only with these supplements can the diet be nutritionally complete.

CALCULATING THE DIET

1. *Age and Weight.* Fill out the following information:

    Age _____
    Ideal weight in kilograms _____
    (See discussion on ideal weight)

Mary has been prescribed a 4:1 ketogenic diet. She is four years old and weighs fifteen kilograms (thirty-three pounds), which at fiftieth percentile matches the ideal weight for her age and size.

2. *Calories per Kilogram.* Determine the number of calories per kilogram based on the child's age and ideal weight from the following chart:

Under 1	75–80 Kcal/kg
Ages 1-3	70–75 Kcal/kg
Ages 4–6	65–68 Kcal/kg

Ages 7–10   55–60 Kcal/kg
11 and over   30–40 Kcal/kg or less

Mary, age four, needs 68 Kcal/kg on the ketogenic diet.

3. Total Calories. Determine the total number of calories in the diet by multiplying the child's weight by the number of calories required per kilogram.

Mary, age four and weighing fifteen kilograms, needs a total of 68 x 15 or 1,020 calories per day.

4. Dietary Unit Composition. Dietary units are the building blocks of the ketogenic diet. A 4:1 diet has dietary units made up of four grams of fat to each one gram of protein + carbohydrate. Because fat has nine calories per gram (9 x 4 = 36), and protein and carbohydrate each have four calories per gram (4 x 1 = 4), a dietary unit at a 4:1 diet ratio has 36 + 4 = 40 calories. The caloric value and breakdown of dietary units vary with the ketogenic ratio:

Ratio	Fat	Calories	Carbohydrate plus Protein	Calories	Calories per Dietary Unit
2:1	2 g x 9 Kcal/g = 18		1 g x 4 Kcal/g = 4		18 + 4 = 22
3:1	3 g x 9 Kcal/g = 27		1 g x 4 Kcal/g = 4		27 + 4 = 31
4:1	4 g x 9 Kcal/g = 36		1 g x 4 Kcal/g = 4		36 + 4 = 40
5:1	5 g x 9 Kcal/g = 45		1 g x 4 Kcal/g = 4		45 + 4 = 49

Mary's dietary units will be made up of 40 calories each because she is on a 4:1 ratio.

5. Dietary Unit Quantity. Divide the total calories allotted (Step 3) by the number of calories in each dietary unit (Step 4) to determine the number of dietary units to be allowed daily.

Each of Mary's dietary units on a 4:1 ratio contains 40 calories, and she is allowed a total of 1,020 Kcal/day, so she gets 1,020/40 = 25.5 dietary units per day.

6. Fat Allowance. Multiply the number of dietary units by the units of fat in the prescribed ketogenic ratio to determine the grams of fat permitted daily.

On her 4:1 diet, with 25.5 dietary units/day, Mary will have 25.5 x 4 or 102 grams of fat per day.

7. *Protein + Carbohydrate Allowance.* Multiply the number of dietary units by the number of units of protein + carbohydrate in the prescribed ketogenic ratio, usually one, to determine the combined daily protein + carbohydrate allotment.

On her 4:1 diet, Mary will have 25.5 x 1 or 25.5 grams of protein + carbohydrate per day.

8. *Protein Allowance.* To maintain health, a four-year-old child should eat a minimum of one gram of protein for every kilogram of weight. On a 4:1 ratio, a child should get just this minimum of protein. On a 5:1 ratio, only .75 grams of protein per day may fit in, so the time period on this ratio should be limited. Higher protein intake is possible on 3:1 or 2:1 diets. The Recommended Dietary Protein Allowance varies with the age of the child.

At fifteen kilograms, Mary should eat 15 grams of protein per day out of her total protein + carbohydrate allowance of 25.5 grams.

9. *Carbohydrate Allowance.* Determine carbohydrate allowance by subtracting protein from the total carbohydrate + protein allowance (Step 7 minus Step 8 above). Carbohydrates are the diet's filler and are always determined last.

Mary's carbohydrate allowance is 25.5 – 15 = 10.5 grams of carbohydrate daily.

10. *Meal Order.* Divide the daily fat, protein, and carbohydrate allotments into three equal meals. Daily food intake can also be divided into four equal meals if necessary. It is essential that the proper ratio of fat to protein + carbohydrate be maintained at each meal.

Mary's diet order reads:

	Daily	**Per Meal**
Protein	15.0 g.	5.0 g.
Fat	102.0 g.	34.0 g.
Carbohydrate	10.5 g.	3.5 g.
Calories	1,020	340

11.   Liquids. Multiply the child's ideal weight by about sixty-five to determine the daily cubic centimeters allotment of liquid. As few as 60 cc. per kilogram may be adequate for an inactive child, but as many as 70 cc. may be needed for an active child in a hot climate. The number of calories in the daily diet is the maximum number of cubic centimeters of liquid that we usually allow. Liquid intake should be spaced throughout the day with no more than 120–150 cc. being given at any one time. Liquids should be noncaloric, such as water, herbal or decaffeinated tea, or decaffeinated sugar-free diet soda. Sugar-free diet soda should be limited to no more than one calorie per day. In hot climates the cream may be excluded from the fluid allowance (in other words, liquids may be increased by the volume of the cream in the diet). The liquid allotment may also be set equal to the number of calories in the diet.

Mary, who lives in Baltimore and gets 1,020 calories per day on the diet, is allowed between 975 and 1,020 cc. of fluid per day, including her allotted cream.

12.   Dietary Supplements. Every child on the ketogenic diet should take a daily dose of 600–650 mg. of oral calcium in a sugar-free form, such as Rugby's calcium gluconate, and a sugarless multivitamin with iron, such as Poly-Vi-Sol liquid or drops.

Sample Calculation

1. Jeremy, a nine-year-three-month-old boy, is to be placed on a 4:1 ketogenic diet. His actual weight is 32 kg. and his height is 134 cm. According to the standard charts, he is at 50 percent for height but 90 percent for weight. His ideal weight is estimated at *29 kg.*

2. Jeremy's total calorie allotment is found by multiplying his ideal weight by 60, the calorie per kg. level recommended for a nine-year-old: 29 x 60 = *1,740 calories per day.*

3. Each of Jeremy's dietary units will consist of
    4 g. fat (x 9 calories per g.) = 36 calories
    1 g. carbohydrate + protein (x 4 calories per g.) = 4 calories
    Total calories per dietary unit = *40 calories*

4. Jeremy's dietary units will be determined by dividing his total daily calorie allotment (Step 2) by the calories in each dietary unit: 1,740 calories/40 calories per dietary unit = *43.5 dietary units per day.*

5. Jeremy's daily fat allowance is determined by multiplying his dietary units (Step 4 above) by the fat component in his diet ratio (4 in a 4:1 ratio): 43.5 x 4 = *174 g. fat.*

6. Jeremy's protein needs are one gram of protein per kilogram of body weight. His ideal weight is 29 kg., so he needs *29.0 g. protein daily.*

7. Jeremy's daily carbohydrate allotment is determined by multiplying his dietary units (Step 4 above) by the 1 in his 4:1 ratio, then subtracting his necessary protein (Step 6 above) from the total: 43.5 − 29 = *14.5 g. carbohydrate per day.*

Jeremy's complete diet order will read:

	Per Day	**Per Meal**
Protein	29.0 g.	9.7 g.
Fat	174.0 g.	58.0 g.
Carbohydrate	14.5 g.	4.8 g.
Calories	1,740	580

CALCULATING MEAL PLANS

Once the diet order is calculated, the next step is to translate it into actual, edible meals.

Traditionally, meal plans have been calculated by hand, using the system of exchange lists and average food values. The computer program allows for greater speed and accuracy, but if you do not have access to a computer, a meal program derived by the hand-calculation process described in this chapter will be equally effective. The diet usually starts with six basic meal plans. When parents call the dietitian to discuss meal plans, they can easily refer to these basic meals by number:

1. Meat/fish/poultry, fruit, fat, cream.

2. Cheese, fruit, fat, cream.
3. Egg, fruit, fat, cream.
4. Meat/fish/poultry, vegetables, fat, cream.
5. Cheese, vegetables, fat, cream.
6. Egg, vegetables, fat, cream.

AVERAGE FOOD VALUES FOR HAND CALCULATIONS*

	Grams	Protein	Fat	Carbohydrate
36% Cream	100	2.0	36.0	3.0
Meat/Fish/Poultry	100	23.3	16.7	0.0
10% Fruit	100	1.0	0.0	10.0
Group B Vegetable	100	2.0	0.0	7.0
Fat	100	0.0	74.0	—
Bacon	100	33.3	41.7	—
Egg	100	12.0	12.0	—
Cheese	100	30.0	35.3	—
Cottage Cheese (4%)	100	13.2	4.4	3.5
Cream Cheese	100	6.7	33.3	3.3
Peanut Butter	100	26.0	48.0	22.0
Strained Meat/Poultry	100	13.3	6.7	—

* Numbers have changed since previous edition.

CROSS MULTIPLICATION: THE KEY TO USING THE FOOD LIST

Question: If 100 g. 36% cream contains 3.0 g. carbohydrate, how much cream contains 2.4 g. of carbohydrate?

Step 1: $\dfrac{100}{3} = \dfrac{X}{2.4}$

Step 2: $3X = 240$

Step 3: $X = 240/3 = 80$ g.

Answer: 80 g. of 36% cream contains 2.4 g. of carbohydrate.

●●●

Calculating a Meal

1. Calculate the whipping cream first. Heavy whipping cream should take up no more than half of the carbohydrate allotment in a meal.

2. Calculate the rest of the carbohydrates (fruit or vegetables) by subtracting the carbohydrate contained in the cream from the total carbohydrate allotment.

3. Calculate the remaining protein (meat/fish/poultry, cheese, or egg) by subtracting the protein in the cream and vegetables from the total protein allowance. The total amount of protein may occasionally be off by 0.1 g. (over or under) without adverse effect.

4. Calculate the amount of fat to be allowed in the meal by subtracting the fat in the cream and protein from the total fat allowance.

Jeremy's Tuna Salad

1. Jeremy is allowed a total of 4.8 g. carbohydrate per meal. To use half of this allotment as cream, he should eat 80 g. of 36% cream, which contains 2.4 g. of carbohydrate.

2. For his remaining 2.4 g. of carbohydrate, Jeremy can eat 35 g. of Group B vegetables, or twice as many Group A vegetables.

3. The 34.3 g. Group B vegetables and 80 g. 36% cream contain a total of 2.3 g. protein. Jeremy is allowed 9.7 g. protein per meal, so he can eat as much tuna as contains 9.7 − 2.3 = 7.4 g. protein. Referring to the food values chart, this works out to be 32 g. tuna.

4. Jeremy has to eat 58 g. fat with each meal. The cream and tuna contain 34.1 g. fat, leaving 32 g. of mayonnaise to be mixed in with his tuna fish.

To determine how many grams of each food item should be included in a given meal, follow these steps:

CALCULATING MEAL PLAN 4

	Weight	**Protein**	**Fat**	**Carbohydrate**
Tuna	32 g.	7.4 g.	5.3g.	—
Group B Vegetable	35 g.	0.7 g.	—	2.4
Fat	32 g.	—	23.9 g.	—
36% Cream	80 g.	1.6 g.	28.8 g.	2.4 g.
Actual Total		9.7 g.	58.0 g.	4.8 g.
Should Be		9.7 g.	58.0 g.	4.8 g.

The 4:1 ketogenic ratio of this menu may be double-checked by adding the grams of protein + carbohydrate in the meal and multiplying by 4. The result should be the amount of fat in the meal, in this case 58 g. Since (9.7 + 4.8) x 4 = 58, the ratio is correct.

• •

NOTES ON JEREMY'S LUNCH

- Jeremy likes his cream frozen in an ice cream ball (slightly whipped), flavored with vanilla and saccharin, and sprinkled with a little cinnamon.
- Jeremy's mom arranges the vegetables in thin-sliced crescents or shoestring sticks around the tuna.
- If Jeremy doesn't like as much mayonnaise with his tuna, some of his fat allowance in the form of oil, perhaps 15 g., can be whipped into the cream one hour after it goes into the freezer. The fats on the exchange list can be used interchangeably—a meal's fat can be provided as all mayonnaise, half mayonnaise and half butter, or half oil and half butter, depending on the child's taste and what makes food sense. In the case of hiding fat in ice cream, oil works nicely because it is liquid and has little flavor.

QUESTIONS AND ANSWERS

1. How do you add extra ingredients to a meal plan when calculating by hand?

Take the tuna salad as an example. Suppose Jeremy wants to sprinkle baking chocolate shavings on his ice cream and bacon bits on the tuna salad. You would add a line for bacon and a line for baking chocolate in your hand or computer calculation. Then choose a small quantity, perhaps five grams of bacon and two grams of baking chocolate, and fill in the values for protein, fat, and carbohydrate of each. The quantities of other ingredients would then have to be juggled downward until all the columns add up to the proper totals. Bacon, which contains protein and fat, will take away from the meal's tuna and mayonnaise allotment. Baking chocolate, which is primarily carbohydrate, will take away from the amount of tomatoes in the meal. As the overall carbohydrate allotment is very small and the nutritive value of chocolate is less than that of vegetables, no more than two grams of chocolate should be used in a meal on the 4:1 ratio. With the accompanying computer program, an additional ingredient may simply be filled in on a blank line, and the other ingredients juggled by eye until the actual totals match the correctly prescribed ones.

2. Do calories have to be reduced when a child turns four or seven, passing into a new calorie-intake category?

Once a child is started on the diet, changes in the diet order are usually made only in response to the child's own performance—weight loss or gain, growth in height, seizure control difficulties, etc.—and not so much to outside factors such as age. If a child is doing well on the diet, we do not change anything for at least a year. After a year we evaluate and may make adjustments based on whether the child has grown, whether any weight loss or gain has occurred, whether the child is still having seizures and, if so, whether there is any more we can do to control them.

3. What if a child on the diet experiences a growth spurt?

As mentioned previously, if a child is doing well on the diet usually nothing should be changed for a full year. Then, if a child has grown, you may want to consider raising calories commensurately. Calories should be liberalized (or restricted) in increments of no more than 100–200 calories per day. Any time calories are raised, the family should be alert for breakthrough seizure activity. If seizures occur at a higher calorie level, it makes sense to limit calories again, even if that means the child may be a bit skinny until the end of the diet. Growth will catch up after the child returns to eating normal food.

4. Must a child always eat three meals a day?

We recommend that meals be divided equally, but a child may eat four equal meals a day if necessary. Four meals might be appropriate for very young children or for those who feel very hungry on the diet and have difficulty tolerating the time between three meals even though they are not losing weight or manifesting any physical indication that the calorie level is low. Snacks, other than the one or two olives or nuts allowed as free food, are generally used as a stopgap measure to provide extra calories to children who are losing weight, and not as a regular feature of the diet. A snack may be useful in testing how many additional calories a child needs, and whether the extra calories cause any seizure activity problems, before that child's entire set of meal plans is recalculated.

5. Is it really necessary to use half of the carbohydrate allotment as cream?

A child on a 3:1 ratio would have to eat a lot of cream if it was calculated to make up half of the carbohydrate allotment. For larger children or those on a 3:1 ratio, the cream should probably be less than half of the carbohydrate allotment for the menu to be palatable; more meat and vegetables can fill in the protein and carbohydrate requirements, and also more fat in the form of mayonnaise, butter, or oil. Although the system for calculating a meal plan is meant as a guideline for an average child, in reality no child is average; every child is an individual. In practice, the diet must make food sense in addition to mathematical correctness in order to be accepted.

A Diet Order Test

Lily is twenty-four months old and weighs twelve kilos. She is 86.5 cm. tall. Both her height and weight are at the fiftieth percentile. She is going to start on a 4:1 ketogenic diet. What will her diet order read?

1. At age two years, Lily's calorie per kilogram requirement will be 75 calories per kilogram. Her ideal weight is the same as her actual weight, twelve kilograms. So Lily's total calorie allotment is 75 x 12 = *900 calories per day.*
2. Lily's dietary units will consist of 40 calories each, the standard for a 4:1 diet.

3. Lily's dietary units are determined by dividing her total calorie allotment by the calories in each dietary unit. So she will have 900/40 = *22.5 dietary units per day.*

4. Lily's daily fat allowance is determined by multiplying her dietary units (22.5) by the fat component in her ratio (4 in a 4:1 ratio). She will thus be allowed 22.5 x 4 = *90 g. fat per day.*

5. Lily's protein + carbohydrate allotment is 22.5 g. per day, determined by multiplying her dietary units (22.5) by the 1 in her 4:1 ratio. Her weight is 12 kg., so allowing one gram of protein per kilogram per day makes her *protein allotment 12 g. per day.*

6. Lily's daily carbohydrate allotment is determined by subtracting her protein allotment (12 g.) from the total protein + carbohydrate allowance (22.5 g.): 22.5 – 12 = *10.5 g. carbohydrate per day.*

Lily's complete diet order will read:

	Per Day	**Per Meal**
Protein	12.0 g.	4.0 g.
Fat	90.0 g.	30.0 g.
Carbohydrate	10.5 g.	3.5 g.
Calories	900	300

A Meal Test

For dinner, Lily would like to eat grilled chicken with fruit salad and a vanilla popsicle. How would you calculate this meal?

1. Always work from the per-meal diet order. Lily is allowed a total of 3.5 g. carbohydrate per meal. To use half of this allotment as 36% cream, her popsicle should contain 57 g. cream, which will provide 1.7 g. carbohydrate.

2. To provide her remaining 1.8 g. carbohydrate, she can have 18 g. of 10% fruit.

3. The 10% fruit and 36% cream contain a total of 1.4 g. protein. Lily's total protein allotment for the meal is 4 g., so she can eat as much grilled chicken as will provide 4 – 1.3 = 2.7 g. protein. This works out to 11 g. chicken.

4. Lily is allowed 30 g. of fat in each meal. The chicken and cream contain a total of 22.6 g. fat. Lily should eat 10 g. of butter or mayonnaise to provide the additional 7.4 g. fat allotment.

Lily's dinner plan will read:

CHICKEN CUTLET WITH FRUIT SALAD

	Weight	Protein	Fat	Carbohydrate
Chicken	11.0 g.	2.6 g.	1.8 g.	—
10% fruit	18.0 g.	0.2 g.	—	1.8 g.
Fat	10 g.	—	7.4 g.	—
36% Cream	58.0 g.	1.2 g.	20.8 g.	1.7 g.
Actual Total		4.0 g.	30.0 g.	3.5 g.
Should Be		4.0 g.	30.0 g.	3.5 g.

Notes on Lily's meal: The chicken can be pounded very thin to make it look bigger on the plate. The fruit salad will be pretty if composed of small chunks of water-packed canned peaches and fresh strawberries. Lily thinks it is fun to pick up the chunks with a toothpick. The cream can be diluted with some allotted water, sweetened with saccharin, flavored with four or five drops of vanilla, and frozen in a popsicle mold in advance of the meal. Lily loves butter; she will eat it straight or it can be spread over her chicken. A small leaf of lettuce can be added to the meal for extra crunch.

Liquid Formulas and Tube Feedings

TEN

INTRODUCTION

Children with seizures have all the same nutritional requirements as other children, but some have special needs when it comes to feeding. The ketogenic diet can be modified to meet the needs of all children, whether they are bottle-fed infants, small children making the transition from bottle to strained food, or children with special feeding problems, such as constant seizures that inhibit chewing or physical problems that prevent swallowing. The ketogenic diet can be formulated in any texture—liquid, soft, solid, or a combination—and can be used even by children who need to be fed by nasogastric or gastrostomy tube.

Soft or liquid diets need only be temporary in some cases. If seizures are so severe that children are unable to chew or swallow properly, and if the ketogenic diet is able to decrease or halt the seizures, they can often begin to chew and swallow and then progress to solid food. They may become more alert, perhaps learning to talk and making progress in other ways that would have seemed impossible before the diet!

CALCULATING BOTH SOFT AND LIQUID DIETS

The process of calculating the basic diet order, of establishing calorie levels and the grams of fat, protein, and carbohydrate permitted on the ketogenic diet, is the same regardless of the consistency of the food.

The first steps in calculating ketogenic diets of either liquid or soft consistency are the same as those used in calculating a traditional ketogenic diet; follow the process described in Chapter 9 or use the computer program. Determine what ideal weight and calorie level per kilogram to plug into the formula, and the proper ketogenic ratio. Then calculate the grams of fat, protein, and carbohydrate per meal an individual child needs. Inactive children may need fewer calories per kilogram than average.

Example: Emily is a thirteen-month-old girl who has been fed by gastrostomy tube since she was eight months old because of intractable seizures and heavy medication. Note that because she is so young Emily will be started on a 3:1 diet ratio. At this age she should get 1.5 g. protein for each kilogram of weight rather than the 1 g. protein per kilo given to older children.

Emily's age	13 months
Height	29.7" (76 cm.), 50th percentile
Actual weight	25 lb (11.4 kg.), 95th percentile
Ideal weight	21.5 lb (9.8 kg.), 50th percentile
Calories/kg	80
Protein requirement	1.5 g. per kg. of body weight
Ketogenic ratio	3:1

Using the above numbers in the formula described in Chapter 9, calculate the diet order via the following steps:

1. *Calories:* 80(Kcal/kg) x 9.8(kg. ideal weight) = *784 calories per day*
2. *Dietary unit:* 784(Kcal)/31(Kcal/dietary unit) = *25.3 units per day*
3. *Fat allowance:* 3 (as in 3:1) x 25.3 (dietary units) = *75.9 g. fat*
4. *Protein:* 1.5 (grams per kg. ideal weight) x 9.8 = *14.7 g. protein*
5. *Carbohydrate:* 25.3 (protein + carbohydrate) – 14.7 (protein) = *10.6 g. carbohydrate*

Per the above calculations, Emily's daily diet order, which will be divided into the number of meals or bottles she regularly gets in a twenty-four-hour period, will read:

	Daily
Protein	14.7 g.
Fat	75.9 g.
Carbohydrate	10.6 g.
Calories	784

PREPARING SOFT DIETS OR TUBE FEEDINGS

Soft diets and tube feedings are used both for babies making the transition from formula to solid food and for children who need to be fed through a tube. Preparing the ketogenic diet in the form of soft, ground, or strained foods is really a question of texture rather than of theory since the basic technique for formulating a soft-diet meal plan for tube feedings is the same as for solid foods. Commercial baby foods, like all commercially processed foods, should be checked to ensure that there are no added sugars.

At first I would mix all the food together, pour it down the tube, and then pour down the water. Then I figured out that food went down more easily if I mixed water in first to loosen it up. Some other tricks I learned:

- Mayonnaise goes down the tube pretty easily when it is warmed up slightly in the microwave and mixed with a little water. Oil and butter or margarine leave a residue on the tube that is difficult to clean, so I always use mayonnaise for the fat.
- As Gerber is the most finely strained baby food you can get, it goes down easier than other strained foods.
- For tube feedings I use Group B vegetables or 15 percent fruit. They have less volume so they are easier to get down. If I am feeding her by mouth, I try to use Group A vegetables—carrots, green beans, or squash—to get more bulk.
- Making the transition to chewing is difficult on the ketogenic diet because you cannot give your child a cracker or cookie to practice chewing on. So in order to slowly introduce texture, I mix my own pureed vegetables, which are a lot chunkier, with part of the Gerber vegetables.

Before she started the diet the doctors thought she'd never be able to eat by mouth, but since her seizures are so much better now I think she'll get off the tube altogether when she's finished with the diet.

—MH

Soft diets for children making the transition from liquid to solid foods, those using gastrostomy tubes, or those who have special chewing problems are based on an exchange list of commercial strained meats, fruits, and vegetables comparable to the exchange list for the regular diet.

EXCHANGE LIST FOR COMMERCIAL BABY FOOD*

FRUIT

10 Percent (Use amount prescribed)	15 Percent (Use 2/3 amount prescribed)
Pineapple	Apple raspberry
Applesauce	Banana with tapioca
Applesauce and apricots	Peaches
Applesauce and pineapple	

VEGETABLES

Group A (Use twice amount prescribed)	Group B (Use amount prescribed)
Carrots	Peas
Green beans	Mixed vegetables
Squash	Beets
Garden vegetables	

STRAINED MEAT

Beef	Chicken
Turkey	Lamb
Pork	Veal
Ham	

*At Johns Hopkins we usually use Gerber strained baby food.

In a soft diet, vegetables, fruits, and meats ground after cooking are combined with heavy cream and fats already in soft or liquid form. Naturally soft foods may also be included, such as:

- cottage cheese;
- cream cheese;
- eggs softened with cream;
- cheese grated and melted with butter.

Preparing Liquid Feedings

The ketogenic diet in liquid form is used primarily for infants and small children making the transition to strained or solid food. Infants under one year of age are not often placed on the ketogenic diet because they may have a difficult time maintaining ketosis. In cases of severe, intractable epilepsy, however, the diet may be tried in children too young to take solid food.

As mentioned previously, we have found that very young children, those under about fifteen months, do better on 3:1 or 3.5:1 ratios than on 4:1 ratios because of their greater amount of body fat, so liquid feedings are usually calculated in this ratio. Otherwise, the process of calculating allotted protein, carbohydrate, and fat is the same for liquid diets as for diets of other consistencies.

Liquid ketogenic diets are most often composed of three ingredients:

- Ross Carbohydrate-free Concentrate (RCF)
  — Soy-based protein, avoids symptoms of cow's milk sensitivities
  — Available through Ross in a concentrated liquid: 13 fluid ounce cans; 12 per case; No. 108
- Microlipid
  — A safflower-oil emulsion that mixes easily in solution; made by Sherwood Medical
  — Rich source of polyunsaturated fat and high in linoleic acid
  — Available in 120 ml bottles; 24 per case; product code 8884-300400
  — Toll-free customer service number: 1-800-428-4400
- Polycose (Glucose Polymers)
  — Source of calories derived solely from carbohydrate
  — Available through Ross in powder form (350 gram cans); 6 per case; No. 746.

Note: All mixed formula should be discarded at the end of the day and opened containers of RCF and Microlipid should be stored in the refrigerator and used within forty-eight hours.

Sugarless multivitamins with iron, calcium supplements, and sterile water are added to complete the mixture, which is described in more detail later in this chapter.

FOOD VALUES FOR LIQUID DIET CALCULATION

	Quantity	Protein	Fat	Carbohydrate
RCF concentrate	100 cc.	4.0 g.	7.2 g.	—
Microlipid	100 cc.	—	50.0 g.	—
Oil	100 g.	—	97.1 g.	—
Polycose powder	100 g.	—	—	94.0 g.

Microlipid, because it is emulsified, mixes much more easily with the other ingredients than oil would, which is why we recommend it. But Microlipid is also more expensive than corn or canola oil. For larger children, or when expense is a factor, vegetable oil may be used. MCT oil may also be substituted, although it is even more expensive than Microlipid.

To set up a liquid meal plan:

1. *Calculate the amount of RCF needed to satisfy the child's protein requirement by cross multiplying.*

Emily's ideal weight is 9.8 kilograms. Her protein requirement is 1.5 g. per kilogram of ideal body weight, or 1.5 x 9.8 = 14.7 g. per day. 100 g. of RCF formula contains 4.0 g. of protein. Use the following formula:

$$\frac{100}{4.0} = \frac{X}{14.7} = \frac{100 \times 14.7}{4.0} = 368 \text{ cc.}$$

Emily will need 368 cc. RCF concentrate to meet her 14.7 g. protein requirement.

2. *Calculate the fat in RCF by cross multiplying, and calculate enough Microlipid to make up the difference.*

   100 g. RCF contains 7.2 g. fat. Emily's 368 cc. of RCF contains:

   $$\frac{100}{7.2} = \frac{368}{X} = \frac{368 \times 7.2}{100} \quad \text{or 26.5 g. fat.}$$

   Subtract the 26.5 g. fat from the total 75.9 g. fat needed (75.9 − 26.5 = 49.4). Remaining fat is 49.4 g.

3. *To calculate the Microlipid needed to make up the remaining 49.4 g. fat in Emily's diet, cross multiply.*

   100 cc. Microlipid contains 50 g. fat. To get 49.4 g. fat, Emily will need:

   $$\frac{100}{50} = \frac{X}{49.4} \quad \text{or} \quad \frac{100 \times 49.4}{50} \quad \text{or 99 cc. Microlipid.}$$

4. *Calculate an amount of Polycose powder sufficient to meet Emily's carbohydrate requirement.*

   100 g. Polycose powder contains 94.0 g. carbohydrate. Emily needs 11 g. Polycose powder to provide her required 10.6 g. carbohydrate, determined by the following formula:

   $$\frac{100}{94} = \frac{X}{10.6} \quad \text{or} \quad \frac{100 \times 10.6}{94} \quad \text{or 11.3.}$$

5. *The liquid allotment is derived by diluting the formula to a concentration of 1 calorie per cc. To calculate the cubic centimeters of sterile water needed to dilute a formula to 1 calorie per cc., add the quantities of all the above liquid ingredients and subtract them from the total number of allotted calories.*

   Emily's RCF and Microlipid total 467 cc. Her total calorie allotment was 784, so she will need 317 (784 − 467) cc. of sterile water mixed in to dilute her formula to 1 calorie per cc.

EMILY'S DAILY FORMULA

		Protein	Fat	Carbohydrate
RCF concentrate	368 cc.	14.7 g.	26.5 g.	—
Microlipid	99 cc.	—	49.4 g.	—
Polycose powder	11 g.	—	—	10.6 g.
Sterile water	317 cc.	—	—	—
Total	**784 cc.**	**14.7 g.**	**75.9 g.**	**10.6 g.**

PREPARATION OF KETOGENIC LIQUID FORMULA

1. Measure RCF concentrate and Microlipid in a graduated cylinder.
2. Weigh Polycose powder on a gram scale and blend with above ingredients.
3. Add allotted sterile water. Shake or stir.
4. Add sugar-free vitamin supplements such as:
   - Ross liquid Vi-Daylin Plus Iron or MeadJohnson, or
   - Poly-Vi-Sol with iron (liquid or drops) and
   - 600 to 650 mg. crushed calcium gluconate tablet. Shake or stir thoroughly.
5. Divide into the number of equal feedings the child will receive in a twenty-four-hour period and refrigerate, or refrigerate full amount and divide into individual portions at feeding time.
6. Bring to room temperature before feeding.

Liquid feedings may also be given as continuous drip tube feedings or through a gastrostomy tube. The tubes may be flushed with 10–15 cc. of sterile or tap water, but no more than this because of the diet's fluid restrictions.

As children are able to tolerate strained foods, the liquid diet may be combined with strained or soft meals. The Polycose powder may also be deleted from the liquid formula and replaced by applesauce or strained baby food (fruits or vegetables) when tolerated.

CONCLUSION

If this book causes one child to avoid having a seizure or becoming toxic on high doses of medication, let alone being permanently cured of previously uncontrollable epilepsy, we will have achieved one of our goals. Having witnessed its success at the Pediatric Epilepsy Center at Johns Hopkins, we know how effective the ketogenic diet can be. If we can make it available to increasing numbers of children at medical centers across the country and beyond, through improved documentation and the ease of calculating it by computer, another goal will have been realized.

The ketogenic diet can only become more widespread if prejudice and skepticism among professionals and parents are dispelled: prejudice among physicians against "alternative medicine" that does not come in a neat antiseptic package; skepticism among parents about whether the benefits of the diet will be worth the loss of food freedom; anxiety among dietitians about the subtleties of the diet calculation. If this book, the computer program, and the videos help to overcome these fears and prejudices, a third goal will have been surpassed.

But our ultimate goal is more far-reaching. Within the ketogenic diet may lie an as yet undiscovered metabolic key to the puzzle of why seizures and epilepsy occur in the first place. If clinical researchers can begin to unravel the chemical changes that accompany the successful ketogenic diet treatment, using modern medical technology and in vivo techniques, perhaps progress can be made. Perhaps the relationship of the metabolic changes to glucose and fatty acid metabolism in the brain can begin to be identified.

Newly found data based on the study of patients undergoing the diet treatment may help us to understand why the ketogenic diet works, and why glucose appears to interfere with its effectiveness. If we can understand what triggers the electrical riots in the brain that we call epilepsy, and if researchers can decipher how the ketogenic diet brings them to an end, we can possibly discover a medication that will block seizures, ideally with no side effects, just like the diet but without its rigor and sacrifice. Maybe we can learn to bottle or inject this medication. When the further use and study of the ketogenic diet has truly furthered the understanding and prevention of epilepsy, only then can we say that we have fully achieved our goals.

This book has been addressed primarily to parents of younger children. Its success in adolescents remains to be fully tested, but motivation and compliance, rather than the diet itself, appear to be the major impediments. The use and effectiveness of the diet in adults has been studied even less. Perhaps the next edition of the book will have a chapter on these age groups.

The overwhelming enthusiasm of parents who have tried the diet, independent of their own success, has motivated many centers to try to establish programs. We hope that each center, each parent, and each child experiences similar success.

Appendixes

Section IV

Medications

1. GENERAL RULES:

- Find one pharmacist who is willing to become knowledgeable about the ketogenic diet and monitor all medications and pharmaceutical products.
- Daily medications should come from only one laboratory because ingredient concentrations vary among manufacturers.
- Medications should be taken only in the form prescribed, as carbohydrate and sugar concentrations vary from liquids to tablets to caplets even if made by the same manufacturer.
- In the event of emergency room treatment or hospital admission, intravenous solutions should be normal saline, not glucose or lactated ringers. Medications should be given rectally or intravenously whenever possible.
- In the event of a life-threatening emergency, the child's immediate need for stabilization comes first. All medical personnel should be advised about the diet and advised that seizure activity may increase with glucose administration.

2. Sources of Information:

ABBOTT LABORATORIES	1-800-633-9110
BIOCRAFT LABORATORIES	1-201-703-0400
BRISTOL-MEYERS SQUIBB	1-800-321-1335
BURROUGHS WELLCOME	1-800-722-9292
DANBURY LABORATORIES	1-800-356-5790
ELI LILLY LABORATORIES	1-800-545-5979
GLAXO	1-800-833-5743
MCNEIL CONSUMER PRODUCTS	1-215-233-7000
PARKE-DAVIS	1-800-223-0432
PROCTER & GAMBLE	1-800-358-8707
ROCHE LABORATORIES	1-800-526-6367
ROSS PRODUCTS DIVISION	1-614-624-7677
ROXANE LABORATORIES	1-800-848-0120
SMITHKLINE BEECHAM	1-800-BEECHAM
THE UPJOHN COMPANY	1-616-329-8244
WALLACE LABORATORIES	1-609-655-6000
WARNER-CHILCOTT LABORATORIES	1-201-540-2000
WYETH-AYERST LABORATORIES	1-215-688-4400

3. Medications commonly used by children on the ketogenic diet:

The following is not intended to be a comprehensive list. There may be other medications available in each category that contain no sugar, starch, or carbohydrates, and as formulations change, some of the medications listed here may be disallowed in the future. It is important to pay close attention to labeling and to contact the manufacturer in case of doubt. **All medications on these lists contain minimal carbohydrate and may be used with the diet *unless otherwise indicated.* If a medication contains less than one gram of carbohydrate per dose, it need not be calculated into the diet.**

ANTIEPILEPTIC MEDICATIONS

DEPAKOTE (ABBOTT)   125 mg sprinkles—no carbohydrate
                                 (minute amounts of magnesium
                                 stearate in the gel capsule)

Depakote (Abbott) (*cont.*)	125 mg tab—25 mg starch 250 mg tab—50 mg starch 500 mg tab—100 mg starch
Dilantin (Parke-Davis)	30 mg capsule—72 mg sucrose, 2 mg cornstarch, 74 mg lactose 100 mg capsule—55 mg sucrose, 2 mg cornstarch, 57 mg lactose * *Avoid use of Infatabs or liquid preparation* *
Felbamate (Wallace)	400 mg tab—87 mg starch, 40 mg lactose 600 mg tab—130 mg starch, 60 mg lactose * *Suspension—1500 mg/5 ml sorbitol. Do not use.* *
Frezium (experimental)	10 mg tab—107 mg lactose, 30 mg cornstarch, 4.5 mg talc, .75 mg magnesium stearate
Gapapentin (Parke-Davis)	100 mg cap—14.25 mg lactose, 10 mg starch 300 mg cap—42.75 mg lactose, 30 mg starch 400 mg cap—57 mg lactose, 40 mg starch
Mysoline (Wyeth-Ayerst)	50 mg tab—27.7 mg lactose, 4.40 mg starch 250 mg tab—22.4 mg lactose, 12 mg starch Suspension—.75 mg/ml saccharine sodium (this is the only sweetener)
Tegretol (Ciba-Geigy)	200 mg tab—50 mg starch * *Avoid use of the 100 mg chewable or liquid preparation.* *

ZARONTIN (PARKE-DAVIS)   250 mg cap—62.6 mg sorbitol
                           * 250 mg/5 cc suspension—3 grams
                               sugar! Do not use. *

PHENOBARBITAL (DANBURY)   30 mg tabs—1.7 mg sodium starch
                               glycolate

   *** Remember: Formulations may change without notification
from the manufacturer! ***

ANTIBIOTICS

Most antibiotic liquid preparations contain large amounts of sugar or
sugar substitutes. Check with manufacturer. Tablets may be a good alternative. Crushing tablets may destroy the medication, however; check
with pharmacist if tablets must be crushed.

- Septra tablets (Burroughs Wellcome). Single or double strength
- Ampicillin (Squibb). 250 and 500 mg. capsules
- Augmentin (SmithKline Beecham). 250 mg. and 500 mg. white-
  coated tablets or oral suspension powder (not chewable tablets
  or pre-mixed suspension)
- Ceclor (Lilly). 250 mg. capsule (not suspension)
- Ceftin (Glaxo). 125 mg., 250 mg., and 500 mg. tablets
- Erythromycin (Abbott). 250 mg. and 500 mg. film-coated tablets
  or time-release capsule

COUGH AND COLD PREPARATIONS

Most liquid preparations for children contain large amounts of sugar
or sugar substitutes. Children can weather most colds without the use
of over-the-counter medications. Check with the manufacturer if medications are needed. Cold and cough remedies commonly used by children on the ketogenic diet:

- Benadryl Decongestant/Allergy Tablets (Parke-Davis)
- Benadryl Allergy/Sinus/Headache Tablets

- Benadryl Cold/Flu Tablets
- Benadryl/Allergy contains lactose and Dye-Free Allergy contains sorbitol. *Do not use.*
- Comtrex Multi-Symptom Cold & Flu Tablets (Bristol Myers Squibb)
- Diabetic Tussin DM (Hi-Tech Pharmaceutical Co., Inc.). Cough suppressant/expectorant.
- Drixoral Cold & Flu Tablets—12 Hour Formula (Schering Plough). The Cold & Allergy formula contains lactose and sugar. *Do not use.*
- Scot-Tussin DM (Scot Tussin Pharmaceutical Co. 1-800-638-7268)
- Tylenol Cold Gelcaps (McNeil)
- Tylenol PM Caplets

LAXATIVES AND STOOL SOFTENERS

Constipation is a chronic problem for most children on the ketogenic diet. Laxatives, enemas, and to a lesser extent suppositories can cause dependency when used on a regular basis. Whenever possible, try to rely on less invasive measures such as stool softeners and natural bulk fiber. In order for any of these remedies to work effectively, sufficient fluid intake must be maintained. Be sure your child is receiving up to his full fluid restriction and offer fluids at the time of medication administration. In particularly severe cases of constipation, talk to your doctor or dietitian about increasing fluid allowances.

- Cal-Mag, or Calcium/Magnesium Liquid (Whole Life Nutritional Supplements). May be used as stool softener and in place of calcium supplement. 1-800-748-5841.
- Colace Capsules or 1% Solution (Apothecon). Stool softener. Do not use syrup.
- Dulcolax suppositories (CIBA Consumer)
- Fiber-Con Tablets (Lederle). Bulk forming laxative. Reserve for use with older children with severe constipation. Ketone levels may drop when used in small children. Do not use powder formulations (such as Metamucil). These contain 10-20 calories per tablespoon.
- Fleet enema (Fleet). Use only small amount and only occasionally. Can cause dependence.

- Glycerin suppositories
- MCT oil (see p. 110)
- Mineral oil. Laxative that is not absorbed by the body, but may carry essential body nutrients with it during elimination. May be used occasionally.
- Pepto-Bismol Original or Maximum Strength Liquid. Anti-diarrheal. Do not use caplets or chewable tablets.
- Peri-Colace Capsules (Apothecon). Stool softener and laxative. Use only after you have tried regular Colace first.
- Phillips' Milk of Magnesia (original flavor only).

PAIN RELIEVERS

- Aleve Tablets.
- Motrin IB Capsules (Upjohn)
- Nuprin Coated Tablets (Bristol Myers Squibb)
- Tempra (Bristol-Meyers Squibb). Infant drops (*not* tablets or pediatric elixir)
- Tylenol (McNeil). Original flavor infant drops, suppositories, or regular/extra-strength tablets. *Do not use* pediatric elixirs.

VITAMIN AND MINERAL SUPPLEMENTS

Liquid supplements are generally recommended for children under a year to three years of age. For older children, give one and a half to two times the dose or give supplements in tablet form. Iron preparations must be given mixed with food as direct contact with teeth can cause black spots.

- Calcium carbonate (Rugby or Giant). 600–650 mg. tablets.
- Fields of Nature makes many individual vitamin supplements for those children with specific deficiencies.
- Lactaid Drops (McNeil Consumer Products). Caplets contain mannitol. Do not use.
- One-A-Day Essential Multi-Vitamin (tablet form for older children)
- One-A-Day Maximum Multi-Vitamin
- Poly-Vi-Sol Drops with iron. Do not give in tablet form.
- Unicap M (Multi-Vitamin in tablet form)
- Vi-Daylin Drops with iron. Do not give in tablet form.

Toothpastes and Mouthwashes

- Arm & Hammer Dental Care toothpaste
- Listermint mouthwash (Warner-Lambert)
- Plax Dental Rinse—original or mint (Consumer Health Care Group)
- Scope—peppermint/mint/baking soda (Proctor & Gamble)
- Tom's of Maine toothpaste
- Ultra brite toothpaste (Colgate-Palmolive)

MCT Oil

MCT oil can be obtained from MeadJohnson pharmaceuticals at a cost of approximately $80 per quart.

It can also be obtained at from K.C. Enterprises, a distributor for the Ultimate Nutrition Company. The product is called MCT Gold. It may be ordered by contacting 1-800-305-0951. The cost is $17.50/liter plus $5.00 shipping charge.

Johns Hopkins Hospital Nursing Critical Pathways

© THE JOHNS HOPKINS HOSPITAL

DEPARTMENT OF PEDIATRICS
KETOGENIC DIET
CRITICAL PATHWAY

Primary Nurse: _____
Case Manager: _____
Attending: _____
Date Initiated: _____
Date discussed with patient/family: _____

for addressograph plate

	Clinic	Hospital Day 1	Hospital Day 2	Hospital Day 3	Hospital Day 4	Hospital Day 5		
MONITORING/ ASSESSMENT		Neuro checks q 6° **Be alert to S&S of ** hypoglycemia!! OR Medication toxicity Monitor seizure activity # of seizures described on flowsheet Nutrition assessment						
TREATMENTS								

167

	Clinic	Hospital Day 1	Hospital Day 2	Hospital Day 3	Hospital Day 4	Hospital Day 5		
MEDICATIONS	Home routine drugs transition to standard sugar-free antiepileptic drugs *Total meds must have ◄.1gm carbohydrate q day		1) Caltrate 600 or Calcimix 2) Unicap M or Poly-Vi-Sol with iron		Glycerin suppository if no BM since admission			
ACTIVITY	Ad lib as tolerated	Ad lib Child Life to playroom	Child Life Assessment					
DIET	NPO after evening meal except clear diet caffeine-free liquids: water, diet Shasta, weak caffeine-free tea	NPO until ►48 hrs and 4 (+) ketones in urine established (¾ maintenance) 60–70cc kg fluid Orange juice 30cc for CS ►40 if symptoms of hypoglycemia	⅓ total diet × 3 meals (eggnog formula) as per nutrition consult sheet	⅔ total diet × 3 meals (eggnog formula)	Full regular ketogenic diet until discharge (7th meal)	Discharge with travel eggnog (2 meals)		
			*Each change in diet must have order written specifying: * Calories, gms CHO, protein, +fat and ratio (Total per Meal)					
TESTS	AM out-patient EEG if not done in past 6 months	Heme 8, Urinalysis M7, M12 AED levels Lipid profile-(hand carried to lipid lab-m6-110)						

TESTS (cont'd)	✓ Ketones q void Glucose ✓ q6° until ⅔ diet established q2° if ◄40					
CONSULTS	Nutrition consult daily - dietitian Social work consult					
PATIENT TEACHING	Family version of path shared with patient and family Meeting with dietitian - 1p.m. Out-patient clinic appointment History and theory of keto diet Fats, carbohydrates, and proteins Ketogenic vs non-ketogenic potential Components of the diet (i.e., ratio, calories, fluid, etc)	Nutritional history and interview with parents on eating habits (dietitian)	Parents have access to ketogenic diet book and parent teaching tape ☐ Yes ☐ No Parents know how to check urine for ketones ☐ Yes ☐ No Review meal plans and food exchanges Parents assist with planning meals to be eaten during the hospital stay	Meal preparation instruction Review scale and measuring technique Discussion of commercial products that can and cannot be used on diet Label reading: How to find hidden sugars Medication review Continue to discuss meal planning options	Review previous material Answer questions Discuss complications that may occur at home and remedies: nausea/hunger constipation refusal to eat illness, etc. low ketosis lethargy	Role playing with older children What to say when offered food How to tell others about the special diet Importance of not cheating, even once

NAME: _____ DATE: _____

	Clinic	Hospital Day 1	Hospital Day 2	Hospital Day 3	Hospital Day 4	Hospital Day 5
DISCHARGE PLANNING		Parents given meal plans ☐ Yes ☐ No	Parents given meal plans ☐ Yes ☐ No Parents must have scale and graduated cylinder for teaching. ☐ Yes ☐ No			
DISCHARGE PLANNING	Teaching Interactive met ☐ Yes ☐ No		Prescriptions for AEDs, calcium and vitamin supply, urine dip sticks ☐ Yes ☐ No			
EVALUATION OF OUTCOMES		Seizure ☐ Yes ☐ No 4 + Ketones ☐ Yes ☐ No NPO ☐ Yes ☐ No	Seizure ☐ Yes ☐ No 4 + Ketones ☐ Yes ☐ No ⅓ diet ☐ Yes ☐ No	Seizure ☐ Yes ☐ No 4 + Ketones ☐ Yes ☐ No ⅓ diet ☐ Yes ☐ No	Seizure ☐ Yes ☐ No 4 + Ketones ☐ Yes ☐ No ⅔ diet (eggnog) ☐ Yes ☐ No	Seizure ☐ Yes ☐ No 4 + Ketones ☐ Yes ☐ No Full ketogenic diet ☐ Yes ☐ No

EVALUATION OF OUTCOMES (cont'd)

Electrolytes WNL ☐ Yes ☐ No	Child Life Assessment ☐ Yes ☐ No	⅔ diet ☐ Yes ☐ No	Full diet ☐ Yes ☐ No			
Family version of path shared ☐ Yes ☐ No	Social Work Assessment ☐ Yes ☐ No	Follow-up scheduled ☐ Yes ☐ No				
	Parents demonstrate how to check urine for ketones ☐ Yes ☐ No	Parents can demonstrate ability to accurately weigh foods using a gram scale ☐ Yes ☐ No	Parents can write on paper a meal plan with specific foods and weights for several complete days ☐ Yes ☐ No			
	Parents can demonstrate correct use of food exchanges in a sample meal plan ☐ Yes ☐ No	Parents can read a product label and determine whether its use is appropriate for the keto diet ☐ Yes ☐ No	Parents can describe possible complications of the diet and their remedies ☐ Yes ☐ No			
	Parents can calculate total fluid allotment for a given day ☐ Yes ☐ No	Parents have Rx for calcium, anti-epileptic drugs, vitamin supply and urine dip sticks ☐ Yes ☐ No				

Signature Title

	P	P	P	P	P	P	P
Night	A	A	A	A	A	A	A
Day							
Evening							

KETOGENIC DIET Critical Pathway (Department of Pediatrics)

171

Selected References

GENERAL INFORMATION ON EPILEPSY:

Freeman JM, Vining EPG, and Pillas DJ, *Seizures and Epilepsy: A Guide for Parents*. Johns Hopkins University Press, Baltimore. 1990, 1996.

RECENT REFERENCES ON THE EFFECTIVENESS AND ACCEPTABILITY OF THE DIET:

Kinsman SL, Vining EPG, Quaskey SA, Mellits ED, Freeman JM. Efficacy of the ketogenic diet for intractable seizure disorders: review of 58 cases. *Epilepsia* 1992;33:1132–1136.

Ross DL, Swaiman KF, Torres F, Hansen J. Early biochemical and EEG correlates of the ketogenic diet in children with atypical absence epilepsy. *Pediatr Neurol* 1985;1:104–108.

Schwartz RH, Eaton J, Bower BD, AynsleyGreen A. Ketogenic diets in the treatment of epilepsy: short-term clinical effects. *Dev Med Child Neurol* 1989;31:145–151.

Schwartz RM, Boyes S, AynsleyGreen A. Metabolic effects of three ketogenic diets in the treatment of severe epilepsy. *Dev Med Child Neurol* 1989;31:152–160.

Wheless JW. The ketogenic diet: fa(c)t or fiction? *J Child Neurol* 1995; 10: 419–23.

OTHER BOOKS OF INTEREST:

Keith, Haddow M. *Convulsive Disorders in Children: With Reference to Treatment with the Ketogenic Diet.* Little, Brown and Company, Boston. 1963, Chapters 12 & 13.

Lennox, William G. *Epilepsy and Related Disorders.* Little, Brown and Company, Boston. 1960. Vol 2:734–739, 824–832.

Livingston, S. *Living with Epileptic Seizures.* Charles C. Thomas, Springfield, Ill. 1963:143–163.

Livingston, Samuel. *The Diagnosis and Treatment of Convulsive Disorders in Children.* Charles C. Thomas, Springfield, Ill. 1954:213–236.

THE MEDIUM-CHAIN TRIGLYCERIDE (MCT) DIET:

Huttenlocher PR, Wilbourn AJ, Signore JM. Medium-chain triglycerides as a therapy for intractable epilepsy. *Neurology* 1971;21:1097–1103.

Sills MA, Forsyth WI, Haidukwych D. The medium-chain triglyceride diet and intractable epilepsy. *Arch Disease in Childhood* 1986:1169–1172.

Trauner, DA. Medium-chain triglyceride (MCT) diet in intractable seizure disorders. *Neurology* 1985:237–238.

OTHER ARTICLES OF INTEREST:

De Vivo DC, Pagliara AS, Prensky AL. Ketotic hypoglycemia and the ketogenic diet. *Neurology* 1973;23:640–649.

Dodson WE, Prensky AL, De Vivo DC, Goldring S, Dodge PR. Management of seizure disorders: selected aspects. Part II. *J Pediatr* 1976;89:695–703.

Herzberg GZ, Fivush BA, Kinsman SL, Gearhart JP. Urolithiasis associated with the ketogenic diet. *J Pediatr* 1990;117:743–745.

Livingston S, Pauli S, Pruce I. Ketogenic diet in the treatment of childhood epilepsy. *Dev Med Child Neurol* 1977;19:833–834.

Millichap JG, Jones JD, Rudis BP. Mechanism of anticonvulsant action of ketogenic diet. *Am J Dis Child* 1964;107:593–603.

Withrow CD. Antiepileptic drugs. The ketogenic diet: mechanism of anticonvulsant action. In: Glaser GH, Penry JK, Woodbury DM, eds. *Antiepileptic Drugs: Mechanisms of Action.* New York: Raven Press, 1980:635–642.

SELECTED EXPERIMENTAL STUDIES OF THE DIET IN ANIMALS:

Appleton DB, De Vivo DC. An animal model for the ketogenic diet. Electroconvulsive threshold and biochemical alterations consequent upon high-fat diet. *Epilepsia* 1974;15:211–227.

De Vivo DC, Malas KL, Leckie MP. Starvation and seizures. Observations on the electroconvulsive threshold and cerebral metabolism of the starved adult rat. *Arch Neurol* 1975;32:755–760.

Mahoney AW, Hendricks DG, Bernhard N, Sisson DV. Fasting and ketogenic diet effects on audiogenic seizure susceptibility in magnesium deficient rats. *Pharmacol Biochem Behav* 1983;18:683–687.

Food Database

THE EPILEPSY DIET TREATMENT FOOD LIST

Category	Code	Description	Grams	Protein	Fat	Carb	Kcal
BABY	BAPAP	Gerber Apple/Apricot	100	0.22	0.22	11.63	49
	BAPPA	Gerber Apple/Pineapple	100	0.08	0.08	10.08	41
	BAPPL	Strained Apples	100	0.16	0.16	10.94	46
	BAPRA	Gerber Apple/Raspberry	100	0.22	0.15	15.17	63
	BBATA	Gerber Banana Tapioca	100	0.37	0.07	15.26	63
	BBEEF	Strained Beef	100	13.64	5.35	0.00	103
	BBEET	Strained Beets	100	1.33	0.08	7.66	37
	BCARR	Strained Carrots	100	0.78	0.16	6.02	29
	BCHIC	Strained Chicken	100	13.74	7.88	0.10	126
	BGRBE	Strained Green Beans	100	1.33	0.08	5.94	30
	BLAMB	Strained Lamb	100	14.04	4.75	0.10	99
	BMIXV	Strained Mixed Vegetables	100	1.25	0.47	7.97	41
	BPEAC	Strained Peaches	100	0.52	0.15	18.89	79
	BPEAR	Strained Pears	100	0.31	0.16	10.86	46
	BPEAS	Strained Peas	100	3.52	0.31	8.13	49
	BPEPA	Strained Pear/Pineapple	100	0.31	0.08	10.86	45
	BSQUA	Strained Squash	100	0.86	0.16	5.63	27

Category	Code	Description	Grams	Protein	Fat	Carb	Kcal
BABY (cont'd)	BTURK	Strained Turkey	100	15.35	7.07	0.00	125
	BAPBL	Gerber Apple/Blueberry	100	0.22	0.22	16.30	68
DAIRY	CHAM	American Cheese, Kraft/ Land O Lake	100	19.05	23.81	9.52	329
	CHCH	Cheddar Cheese, Kraft/ ' Land O Lake	100	21.43	32.14	3.57	389
	CHCO	Cottage Cheese, 2% Lowfat	100	13.16	2.19	2.63	83
	CHCR	Cream Cheese, Philadelphia Brand	100	6.67	33.33	3.33	340
	CHMON	Monterey Cheese	100	24.64	30.71	0.71	378
	CHMOZ	Mozzarella Cheese, Whole Milk	100	21.43	25.00	3.57	325
	CHPAR	Parmesan, Grated	100	42.00	30.00	4.00	454
	CHSW	Swiss Cheese	100	24.50	24.85	2.10	332
	CHWZ	Cheez Whiz, Kraft	100	16.43	20.36	6.43	275
	CREA1	Cream, 36%	100	2.00	36.00	3.00	344
	CREA2	Cream 30%	100	2.00	30.67	2.67	295
	EGG	Egg, Fresh	100	12.00	9.00	1.20	134
	SOUR	Sour Cream	100	3.33	16.67	6.67	190
	YOGUR	Yogurt, Plain Lowfat	100	5.24	1.54	7.05	63
	CHMOZ2	Mozzarella Cheese, Part Skim	100	28.57	17.86	3.57	289
	CHCO2	Cottage Cheese 4% Lowfat	100	13.16	4.39	3.51	106
	CHRC	Ricotta Cheese, Whole Milk	100	9.68	12.90	6.45	181
	CHRC2	Ricotta Cheese, Part Skim	100	10.34	7.76	6.90	139
	WHMK	Whole Milk (ML)	100	3.39	3.39	5.02	64

FATS

Code	Name					
BUTT	Butter	100	0.67	81.33	0.00	735
MARG	Margarine, Stick Corn	100	0.00	76.00	0.00	684
MAYO	Mayonnaise, Hellman	100	1.43	80.00	0.70	729
OILC	Corn Oil	100	0.00	97.14	0.00	874
OILO	Olive Oil	100	0.00	96.43	0.00	868
OILP	Puritan Oil	100	0.00	100.00	0.00	900
OILM	MCT Oil	100	0.00	92.67	0.00	834

FISH

Code	Name					
FLOU	Flounder, Baked	100	24.12	1.53	0.00	110
HADD	Haddock, Baked	100	24.30	0.95	0.00	106
LOBST	Lobster, Raw	100	18.82	0.94	0.47	86
REDS	Red Snapper, Raw	100	26.35	1.76	0.00	121
SALM	Salmon, Raw	100	20.00	3.41	0.00	111
SCAL	Scallops, Raw	100	16.82	0.71	2.35	83
SHRIM	Shrimp, Raw	100	20.35	1.76	0.94	101
SWORD	Swordfish, Baked	100	25.41	5.18	0.00	148
TROUT	Rainbow Trout	100	26.35	4.35	0.00	145
TUNA1	Tuna Lt Chnk Star Kist/Oil	100	22.41	22.41	0.00	291
TUNA2	Tuna Lt Chnk Star Kist/Water	100	23.21	0.89	0.00	101
TUNA3	Tuna All White Starkist/Water	100	21.43	8.93	0.00	166
TUNA4	Tuna, Fresh	100	29.88	6.24	0.00	175

FRUIT

Code	Name					
APPLE	Apple	100	0.21	0.36	14.84	63
APPLS	Applesauce, Unsweetened	100	0.16	0.08	11.31	47
APRI	Apricot	100	1.42	0.38	11.13	54
BANAN	Banana	100	1.05	0.53	23.42	103
BLUE	Blueberries	100	0.69	0.41	14.14	63

Category	Code	Description	Grams	Protein	Fat	Carb	Kcal
FRUIT (cont'd)	CANT	Cantaloupe	100	0.88	0.25	8.38	39
	CHERR	Cherries	100	1.18	1.03	16.62	80
	FRCOC	Fruit Cocktail Canned/Water	100	0.41	0.08	8.52	36
	GRAFR	Grapefruit, Pink	100	0.57	0.08	7.72	34
	GRAPG	Green Grapes	100	0.65	0.33	17.17	74
	GRAPP	Purple Grapes	100	0.69	0.56	17.75	79
	HONML	Honeydew Melon	100	0.80	0.30	7.70	37
	JAPP	Apple Juice	100	0.10	0.10	11.70	48
	JORAN	Orange Juice	100	0.70	0.20	10.40	46
	LEMON	Lemon	100	1.03	0.34	9.31	44
	LEMRI	Lemon Rind	100	1.67	0.00	16.67	73
	MANGO	Mango	100	0.53	0.29	17.00	73
	NECT	Nectarine	100	0.96	0.44	11.76	55
	ORANG	Orange, Navel	100	1.00	0.07	11.64	51
	PEACH	Peach	100	0.69	0.11	11.15	48
	PEAR	Pear	100	0.42	0.42	15.12	66
	PINEA	Pineapple	100	0.39	0.45	12.39	55
	PLUM	Plum	100	0.76	0.61	13.03	61
	PUMPK	Pumpkin, Canned	100	1.07	0.25	8.11	39
	RASP	Raspberries	100	0.89	0.57	11.54	55
	STRAW	Strawberries	100	0.60	0.40	7.05	34
	TANG	Tangerine	100	0.60	0.24	11.19	49
	WATML	Watermelon	100	0.63	0.44	7.19	35
GENERIC	GMFP	Generic Meat, Fish, Poultry	100	23.30	16.70	0.00	243
	GFRU	Generic 10% Fruit Exchange	100	1.00	0.00	10.00	44

Code	Name					
GVEG	Generic Group B Vegetable Exchange	100	2.00	0.00	7.00	36
GPBUT	Generic Peanut Butter Exchange	100	26.00	48.00	22.00	624
GFAT	Generic Butter, Margarine, Mayo	100	0.00	74.00	0.00	666
GSTMT	Generic Strained Meats	100	13.33	6.67	0.00	113

MEAT

Code	Name					
BACO	Bacon, Oscar Mayer	100	33.33	41.67	0.00	508
BEEF1	Eye Round Beef	100	29.00	6.50	0.00	175
BEEF2	Lean Ground Beef Medium	100	24.20	19.10	0.00	269
BOLO1	Beef Bologna, Oscar Mayer	100	10.71	28.57	3.57	314
BOLO2	Beef Bologna, Hebrew National	100	10.71	10.71	2.86	151
CANBAC	Canadian Bacon, Oscar Mayer	100	19.58	4.17	0.42	118
CORBF	Corned Beef, Oscar Mayer	100	20.00	1.76	0.59	98
HAM	Cured Ham, Center Slice	100	20.20	12.90	0.10	197
HOTD1	Beef Frank, Hebrew National	100	12.50	29.17	2.08	321
HOTD2	Beef Frank Oscar Mayer	100	11.11	28.89	2.22	313
LAMB	Leg of Lamb, Lean	100	28.71	7.06	0.00	178
LEAN	Lean and Tasty	100	23.30	35.80	0.80	419
PORK	Pork Chop, Lean Broiled	100	32.00	10.50	0.00	223
SAUS1	Oscar Mayer Pork, Beef Link	100	13.30	27.80	2.20	312
SAUS2	Sausage, Bob Evans	100	13.57	30.71	2.50	341
SAUS3	Sausage, Hillshire Farm	100	12.28	29.82	3.51	332
VEAL	Veal Cutlet	100	27.06	11.06	0.00	208

MISC

Code	Name					
CHOC1	Baking Chocolate, Bakers	100	11.07	52.14	30.00	634
CHOC2	Baking Chocolate, Hershey's	100	14.29	56.43	23.93	661
COCOA	Hershey's Cocoa	100	27.30	12.80	45.70	407
JELLO	Jello Sugar Free Gelatin	100	1.16	0.00	0.17	5

Category	Code	Description	Grams	Protein	Fat	Carb	Kcal
MISC (cont'd)	MUST1	Mustard Yellow	100	4.00	4.00	6.00	76
	OLIV1	Olives, Green	100	1.09	10.65	1.09	105
	OLIV2	Olives, Black	100	1.67	28.75	7.08	294
	SOY	Soy Sauce	100	10.52	0.17	5.52	66
	TARTA	Tartar Sauce, Kraft	100	0.00	64.29	0.00	579
	VINEG	Vinegar, Distilled	100	0.00	0.00	5.33	21
NUTS	ALMON	Almonds, Dry Roasted	100	16.43	52.50	24.64	637
	BRAZ	Brazil Nuts	100	14.64	67.14	12.86	714
	CASH	Cashews, Dry Roasted	100	15.71	47.14	34.29	624
	MACAD	Macadamia Nuts	100	8.57	75.71	8.93	751
	PEAN1	Peanuts, Dry Roasted	100	23.57	49.64	21.43	627
	PEAN2	Peanuts, Oil Roasted	100	29.64	48.57	16.07	620
	PECAN	Pecans	100	8.21	65.71	22.50	714
	PETE	Peter Pan Chunky Peanut Butter	100	25.00	50.00	22.00	638
	PIST	Pistachio Nuts	100	15.00	53.57	27.86	654
	SKIP	Skippy Creamy Peanut Butter	100	28.13	53.13	15.60	653
	SUNF	Sunflower Seeds	100	23.21	50.36	18.93	622
	WALN	Walnuts, Black, Dried	100	24.64	57.50	12.14	665
POULTRY	CHIC	Chicken Breast—No Skin (Cooked)	100	31.05	3.60	0.00	157
	TURK	Turkey Breast	100	29.90	3.20	0.00	148
SOUP	BOUL1	Wylers Inst Boull—Chicken/Beef	100	0.00	0.00	28.57	114
	BROTH1	Swanson Canned—Chicken (ML)	100	0.83	0,83	0.42	12

Code	Name					
BROTH2	Swanson Canned—Beef (ML)	100	0.83	0.42	0.42	9
BROTH3	Swanson Canned—Vegetable (ML)	100	0.00	10.42	1.25	9
TUBE						
TMICR	Microlipid (ML)	100	0.00	50.00	0.00	450
TPLOY	Polycose Powder	100	0.00	0.00	94.00	376
TRCFC	RCF Concentration (ML)	100	4.00	7.20	0.00	81
VEGETABLE						
ASPAR	Asparagus—C (Grp A)	100	2.56	0.33	4.44	31
BEAN1	Green Beans	100	1.94	0.32	7.90	42
BEET	Beets—C (Grp B)	100	1.06	0.00	6.71	31
BROC	Broccoli—C (Grp B)	100	2.95	0.25	5.50	36
BRUS	Brussels Sprouts	100	2.56	0.51	8.31	48
CABB1	Cabbage, Green—R	100	1.14	0.29	5.43	29
CABB2	Cabbage, Green—C	100	0.93	0.13	4.80	24
CARR	Carrots—R or C (Grp B)	100	1.15	0.13	10.50	48
CATS	Tomato Catsup	100	2.00	0.67	25.33	115
CAUL	Cauliflower—C (Grp B)	100	2.00	0.20	5.00	30
CELE	Celery—R or C (Grp A)	100	0.75	0.25	3.75	20
CHIVE	Chives—R	100	3.33	0.00	3.33	27
CORN	Corn, Yellow	100	3.29	1.34	25.12	126
CUCU	Cucumber—R (Grp A)	100	0.58	0.20	2.90	16
EGGPL	Eggplant—C (Grp A)	100	1.22	0.00	6.34	30
ENDIV	Endive	100	1.20	0.40	3.20	21
KALE	Kale—C (Grp B)	100	1.85	0.46	5.69	34
LETT	Lettuce, Iceberg (Grp A)	100	1.00	0.00	2.00	12
MUSH1	Mushrooms—R	100	2.00	0.57	4.57	31
MUSH2	Mushrooms, Canned	100	1.92	0.26	5.00	30

181

Category	Code	Description	Grams	Protein	Fat	Carb	Kcal
VEGETABLE	MUST	Mustard Greens—C	100	2.29	0.29	2.14	20
(cont'd)	OKRA	Okra—C (Grp B)	100	1.88	0.13	7.25	40
	ONION	Onions, Raw	100	1.13	0.25	7.38	36
	PARSL	Parsley—R	100	2.33	0.33	7.00	40
	PEAS	Green Peas—R	100	5.38	0.38	14.49	83
	PEPP	Green Peppers—R or C (Grp A)	100	0.80	0.40	5.40	28
	PICK	Dill Pickle Slices	100	0.80	0.00	2.30	12
	POTA1	Potato—Boiled w/o Skin	100	1.70	0.07	20.00	87
	POTA2	Potato—Baked w/Skin	100	2.33	0.10	25.25	111
	RADI	Radish—R (Grp A)	100	0.67	0.44	3.56	21
	SAUER	Sauerkraut—C (Grp A)	100	0.93	0.17	4.32	23
	SPIN1	Spinach—R	100	2.86	0.36	3.57	29
	SPIN2	Spinach, Frozen, w/Butter, Pillsbury	100	3.00	1.00	4.40	39
	SPROU	Bean Sprouts, Mung—R	100	3.08	0.19	5.96	38
	SQUAS	Spaghetti Squash	100	0.64	0.26	6.41	31
	TOMA	Tomato, Red—R	100	0.89	0.24	4.31	23
	TOMAC	Tomato, Canned in Puree	100	0.84	0.84	5.04	31
	TOMAP	Tomato Paste, Canned	100	3.82	0.92	18.85	99
	TOMPU	Tomato Puree	100	1.68	0.12	10.04	48
	TOMSA	Prego, Spaghetti Sauce w/Meat	100	2.12	5.13	17.88	126
	TURNI	Turnips, Boiled	100	0.77	0.13	4.87	24
	ZUCCH	Zucchini—C (Grp A)	100	1.23	0.15	2.92	18

About the Authors

DR. JOHN M. FREEMAN is the Lederer Professor of Pediatric Epilepsy, and Professor of Neurology and Pediatrics at Johns Hopkins, where he was also former Director of the department of Pediatric Neurology. He is the director of the Pediatric Epilepsy Center at the Johns Hopkins Medical Institutions. Initially trained at Johns Hopkins, he learned the value of the ketogenic diet from Dr. Samuel Livingston in the late 1950s and has continued to use it ever since. He is an honorary Lifetime Director of the Epilepsy Foundation of America and a member of the Professional Advisory Board of the Epilepsy Association of Maryland. Dr. Freeman is the author of numerous publications about epilepsy in children and the winner of numerous awards.

MILLICENT T. KELLY, R.D., L.D., became intrigued with the ketogenic diet during her dietetic internship at the Johns Hopkins Hospital School of Dietetics in 1948-49. Following graduation she became a nutrition instructor with the Johns Hopkins School of Nursing. She later worked in the Johns Hopkins Hospital's Nutrition Department for twenty-eight years, becoming Dietician In Charge. During this time she became proficient in the use of the ketogenic diet. Now semi-retired, she has continued her association with the Johns Hopkins Pediatric Epilepsy Center, guiding children and parents through the ketogenic diet on a regular basis.

JENNIFER B. FREEMAN is a writer and international business development consultant in New York City. She feels honored to be able to contribute to the well-being of future generations of children with epilepsy.